GU00367391

India Redefines its Role

Contents

Oxford University Press, Walton Street, Oxford OX2 6DP
Oxford New York
Athens Auckland Bangkok Bombay
Calcutta Cape Town Dar es Salaam Delhi
Florence Hong Kong Istanbul Karachi
Kuala Lumpur Madras Madrid Melbourne
Mexico City Nairobi Paris Singapore
Taipei Tokyo Toronto
and associated companies in
Berlin Ibadan

Oxford is a trade mark of Oxford University Press

Published in the United States
by Oxford University Press Inc., New York

© The International Institute for Strategic Studies 1995

First published January 1995 by Oxford University Press for
The International Institute for Strategic Studies
23 Tavistock Street, London WC2E 7NQ

Director: Dr John Chipman

British Library Cataloguing in Publication Data

Data available

Library of Congress Cataloging in Publication Data

ISBN 0-19-828021-1
ISSN 0567-932X

INTRODUCTION

If the 1980s failed to meet expectations of fundamental change in India, the 1990s render change unavoidable. Revolutionary shifts in India's domestic, regional and global environment have obliterated the principles and presumptions that until recently have determined the internal and international politics of the world's most populous democracy. The early 1990s have marked the end of the Nehru–Gandhi dynasty that ruled India for more than four decades, except for minor hiccups of coalition politics, and provided a notion of stability and continuity. This decade has also seen the end of the Congress Party's total domination of national politics. Externally, this coincided with the disappearance of India's most trusted ally, the Soviet Union. Domestically, it underlined the need to bury old Nehruvian political values and the curious philosophical brew of non-alignment, mixed economy and Fabian socialism. At the same time came the rise of Hindu communalism, threatening the very basis of India's secular polity.

The loss of its most significant foreign friend and the dynasty that guided its fortunes for so long is bound to rewrite power equations in the region and change the paradigms that shape India's world view. In the past, India's domestic policies rested on a mixture of Nehru's benign socialism and his daughter Indira Gandhi's cynical but vote-catching populism. Both Indira and later Rajiv Gandhi deviated sharply from Nehruvian methods by over-centralising authority; cutting at the federal roots of the power structure; systematically destroying regional centres of power and leaders, even within their own party; reducing state (province) chief ministers to glorified vassals; and single-mindedly chipping away at democratic institutions, including the judiciary and election commission. Until Rajiv Gandhi's short-lived economic reform of the mid-1980s, 'profit' was a dirty word and taxes were oppressively high. Combined with over-protection and the Byzantine regime of controls often called the 'licence-quota raj', this condemned India to decades of 3–4% growth, the so-called 'Hindu rate of growth'.[1]

Externally, the Nehru–Gandhi dynasty considered foreign, defence and nuclear policies its own preserve, but the moorings of these, and the Indira–Rajiv activist, often interventionist, foreign policy, have gone. It was this latter 'civilian militarism' that enabled India to become a key player in the region, beginning with its intervention in East Pakistan, leading to the creation of Bangladesh in 1971, and culminating in the controversial Rajiv–Jayewardene

3

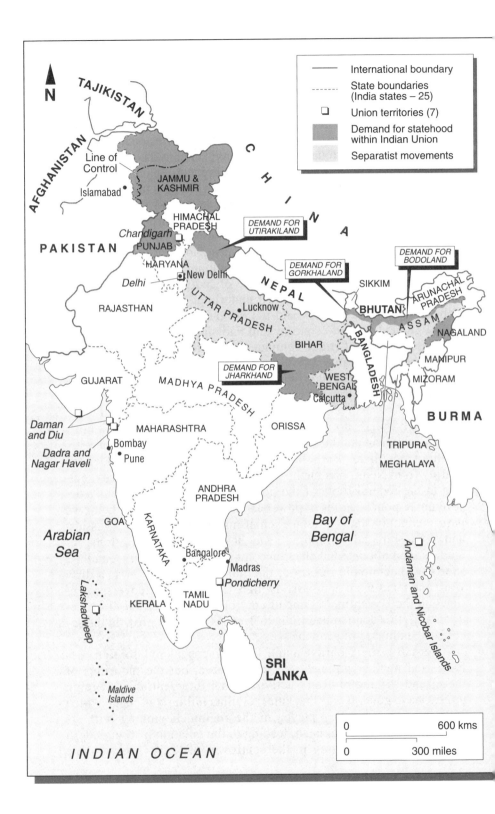

accord under which the Indian Peace-Keeping Force (IPKF) was sent to Sri Lanka in 1987 to help solve its ethnic problem.[2]

It is also time for a major turnaround in defence policies. In the 1980s, assorted factors, such as the fruits of the green revolution, nearly 15 years of peace and offshore oil finds, topped by the emergence of an uncharacteristically aggressive body of military officials, resulted in ambitious power projection and excessive defence spending that broke the self-imposed barrier of 4% of the gross domestic product (GDP) for the first time in 1988–89.[3] This catapulted India among the top arms-importing nations in the world and raised visions of a rapidly mechanising, nuclear-capable army and a blue-water navy. But these ambitions were thwarted by the 1991 bankruptcy that forced India to raise loans from the International Monetary Fund (IMF), necessitating economic restructuring and fulfilment of loan 'conditionalities' requiring defence budget cuts. As the armed forces reel under the dual impact of crippled resources and the unpredictability of the Russian supply line, India is reassessing its security environment, threats and capabilities.

Traditionally, India had a siege mentality, imagining danger from China and Pakistan along its land borders, and suspecting smaller neighbours such as Bangladesh and Nepal of conspiring with its enemies.[4] The 'big power' presence in the Indian Ocean was seen as a threat, and the 5,000km Indian coastline was considered vulnerable to expanding naval capabilities in the region. Globally, India's non-aligned policies invited the censure of the West. Much has changed now, and promises to keep changing. As a consequence of a thaw in relations with China, for the first time in four decades Indian strategists can think in terms of no more than a single-front war. The disappearance of American Cold War partiality for Pakistan has also enabled the US to embark on a more equidistant policy in the subcontinent, although India is still far from satisfied with it. Most significant of all, economic reform and the enthusiasm it has generated have brought international focus to India after many decades of indifference.

Yet too often in the past India has generated hopes and failed to fulfil them. Rajiv Gandhi's youthful promise of taking India into the twenty-first century foundered on charges of corruption. The subsequent secular, issue-based coalition that won power in 1989 by making corruption its major election plank also drowned in maladministration and cynical caste politics. The 1991 election of the somewhat lack-lustre politician P. V. Narasimha Rao followed a particularly inauspicious series of events for India, with the collapse of two governments and yet another election resulting in an unclear verdict. The instability and uncertainty caused by Rajiv Gandhi's assassination during the 1991 election campaign should be seen in this context, given that he was president of the Congress Party, which has ruled the Centre for longer than any other national party. Through a combination of shrewd politics and cynical defections, Rao has attained a real majority and is talking in terms of a second term. But problems remain: the politico-economic change has set in motion new worries and social discord. There are increasing caste tensions in the Hindi-speaking political heartland following the victory of a lower-caste coalition in provincial elections. Several movements are emerging, with varying degrees of popular backing, against economic reform and privatisation of the public sector, as opposition parties from the far left to the far right have jumped on the xenophobic bandwagon. It is with this opposition, nurtured by a long history of anti-colonial politics, that policy-makers will have to contend as they shape policies for a new India.

Indian foreign and security policies have been remarkably consistent. It is ironic that the onus to change them now falls on a government of the Congress Party that instituted and nurtured them. Some pragmatism is already evident: the timely diplomatic opening to Israel and South Africa that reversed the old ideological positions; and the thaw with China, defying fears of a jingoistic reaction. But how much freedom do today's political realities give New Delhi on the crucial issues of nuclear proliferation and Kashmir?

Internally, India has a history of fighting separatist movements with a combination of military, political and constitutional means. The manner in which India has dealt with ethnic, communal and separatist conflicts is of broader interest at a time when there is similar conflict in the international system. With rebellions in the north-western granary of Punjab and the north-eastern tribal states abating, India's internal insecurities should have diminished. But continuing violence in Kashmir, the widening of the Hindu–Muslim schism and vicious caste politics in the Hindi-speaking region will give New Delhi no respite.

Where is India headed in this process of redefining its regional and international identity? Will future leaders jettison ambitions of playing an international role commensurate with India's stature as the developing world's oldest and largest democracy, or will they look for different routes to reach that objective? This paper analyses the complex economic, political, social and external factors, and their likely impact on India's policy and stability.

I. FORCES FOR CHANGE AND INTERNAL STABILITY

Much of the discussion on India's prospects for survival, stability and growth has so far been concentrated on domestic politics with its peculiar complications of caste, religion, language and socio-economic divisions. Foreign and security policies, particularly in the light of the persistent secessionist movements, have entered the debate, but economic policy seems to have been taken for granted as the area where change was least expected. That is why the most important contribution made to India by the Narasimha Rao government is the replacement of political preoccupation with a concern for economics. This is particularly remarkable considering that Rao came to power in a period of great political instability beginning in autumn 1990 with the collapse of the coalition government led by V. P. Singh. Holding no more than 145 seats in the 545-strong Lok Sabha (the Lower House of Parliament), and supported from the 'outside' by the Bharatiya Janata Party (BJP) on the extreme right, and the Communist Party of India (Marxist) on the extreme left, Singh's government was bound to fail. When it did, it left India more vulnerable than it had been for three decades – politically, economically and socially. The coalition government was replaced by a cabinet headed by its breakaway faction, just 52-strong and not even commanding a quorum in Lok Sabha, and yet again supported from 'outside' by Rajiv Gandhi's Congress (I). Predictably, this too collapsed, forcing mid-term elections in 1991. This instability, combined with the military costs of increasing troubles in Punjab and Kashmir, left the country nearly bankrupt. Next came the 1991 Gulf War, raising oil prices and, with the flight of nearly 200,000 Indian expatriate workers, causing disruption in the flourishing money-order economy of India's manpower-exporting regions.

Much has now changed, and although the World Bank may have been a little hasty in hailing Indian and Chinese economic reform as equally significant as the end of the Cold War, the fact is that more than the change in the regional geopolitical situation, the new superpower equations or internal discord, it is economic change that has become the crucial determinant of India's evolution.[1]

With the help of his Finance Minister, Dr Manmohan Singh, Prime Minister Rao has embarked on a major reform of India's economy. Three consecutive budgets and corresponding amendments in trade and commerce legislation have sought to abolish the licence-quota raj. Despite some false starts, and resistance from the bureaucracy, this change has restructured the political agenda of the nation. All the opposition parties, from the BJP on the right, to the Marxists on the left, have had to turn from purely political issues to economic ones. The rewriting of socio-political paradigms is underlined by the rapid growth of business publications in English as well as several Indian languages, while the previously dominant political media have mostly declined or stagnated.[2]

In retrospect, this reform is a blessing of bankruptcy. In summer 1991, foreign-exchange reserves were as low as $1 billion. Facing the unprecedented humiliation of defaulting on debt repayments, India had to sell 90 tonnes of gold from its national reserve to maintain liquidity. Annual inflation peaked at 16.7% in August 1991. India's international credit worthiness was so low that even expatriate Indians began a run on their deposits in Indian banks, despite some of the highest foreign-exchange interest rates in the world. Rao and his new economic think-tank saw in this an opportunity to reverse the faulty old economics, although without making so public a repudiation of the Congress Party's political icons, Nehru and Indira Gandhi.

The old policy had originated in the 1950s.[3] Aimed at poverty removal through capital accumulation, it continued to fail, but each setback was met with further strengthening of controls rather than an admission that the policy itself was defective. Through its banking system and the Controller of Capital Issues, the government controlled all the long- and short-term credit in the country. Meanwhile, the public sector expanded into diverse fields, ranging from wristwatches to fighter jets, television sets to radars, shoes to condoms, soft drinks to penicillin, bread to hotels and restaurants. In aggregate, these produced gargantuan losses, adding up to Rs150bn ($5bn) by 1993, and any profits were misleading.[4] The entire petroleum sector was a government monopoly, its products controlled by administered prices, and it was this that accounted for nearly all the profits in the public sector. The state sector was also riddled with political patronage and nepotism. The 1991 financial crisis forced the Rao government to address the accumulated follies of the past.[5]

If summer 1991 necessitated desperate measures, the subsequent years have seen the emergence of a clear Rao–Manmohan Singh strategy. The rupee has been devalued, controls reduced, clearance of foreign joint ventures simplified, and most quotas have been abolished, virtually freeing captive industries such as steel, cement and sugar. Personal, corporate and excise taxes have been slashed across the board, export profits exempted from tax and exporters allowed to keep a percentage of these in free foreign-exchange ac-

8

counts. Import of gold by non-residents has been permitted at nominal duty, and the harsh 1973 Foreign Exchange Regulation Act (FERA) is being drastically revised.

The results have been mixed, but tend largely towards improvement. Inflation was down in 1993, touching its lowest level in the past 25 years; stock indices have doubled; exports have been rising despite civil disturbances (achieving a 22% increase in 1993–94); foreign-exchange reserves are up more than eighteenfold over the 1991 summer levels and foreign investment is up several times.[6] In 1993–94, Indian companies raised $1.5bn internationally through global depository receipts and began using the money to pay off old, expensive debts. Major international investments have been cleared, despite political opposition in the fields of power, petrochemicals and telecommunications. By early 1994, foreign direct investment had risen nearly 40 times over the Rs2.3bn in 1989 (which was partly historical and consisted mainly of British investment in the plantations).[7] The rupee has remained remarkably stable – in fact, it improved marginally over the 1993–94 period despite large-scale buying of the dollar by the Reserve Bank of India to keep Indian exports competitive. Smuggling of gold and foreign-currency on the blackmarket persists, but at a negligible level compared to the past. Several public-sector undertakings, including the State Bank of India, have sold a part of the equity to the public and liberalisation is becoming apparent even in areas previously guarded jealously by the state, such as civil aviation and broadcasting. In 1992–94, India saw the emergence of nearly a dozen small private airlines competing with the state-run domestic carrier, Indian Airlines. Several independent channels appeared on both the state-run radio in metropolitan towns and television. Electronic media, particularly satellite TV, are also changing social attitudes, bringing into poor and middle-class households images of an affluent West. This could fuel either ambition or frustration, depending on how quickly economic reform yields results.

Democracy And Constraints On Reform
Even if not as radical as in China, these changes are remarkable because of the political compulsions that reformers face in India. A fundamental difference between the uncaging of the Chinese economic tiger and the unshackling of the Indian economic elephant is that India's leaders have not only to deal with general elections every five years, but also frequent elections in states during their term at the Centre. There is also a lively parliament with which to contend,

besides opposition from old socialists within the ruling party and others who find the fence the most prudent place to sit politically. With general elections due in 1996, familiar pressures will return, especially from farmers' leaders, for whom the price of hybrid seeds will increase while fertiliser subsidies will be reduced; from Indian industry, demanding a level playing field; and trade unions, including the Congress Party-run Indian National Trade Union Congress (INTUC), which will oppose privatisation, and (politically the most volatile step) an exit policy for sick industry that allows companies to close down and lay off labour.

The 1994–95 budget reflected these concerns. Dr Manmohan Singh had palliatives for several pressure groups in his business-friendly 1994–95 budget: bowing to populist pressures, he allowed the fiscal deficit to continue. Similarly ambitious plans to privatise India's dinosaur-ridden public sector, and either close down or re-structure loss-making units, ran into strong political headwind. Despite the national Telecom Commission's recommendation for the creation of a corporation in place of the state monopoly, the government retreated because of union pressures. Other examples are the public-sector steel giants Steel Authority of India Ltd (SAIL) and the Indian Iron and Steel Company (IISCO). SAIL is being professionalised slowly in the face of stiff bureaucratic opposition, but plans to sell the ailing IISCO to a well-known private-sector steelmaker created a political storm. Outcry from the trade unions cut across party lines and the government has not been able either to close down the unit or sell it to private buyers.

Concerned about the political fallout, and conscious that his Finance Minister is not a professional politician, Rao is increasingly taking charge of economic changes personally and has unveiled a philosophy of gradualism – firm, but cautious reform. The opposition too has made the economy the main plank in their new agenda, the first item being India's signing of the General Agreement on Tariffs and Trade (GATT). Describing it as a calamitous surrender of sovereignty that would destroy domestic industry, starve the farmer and pauperise the nation, the opposition, from the left to the right, has exploited the issue for political gain. The campaign has found some support, partly because it appeals to deep xenophobic sentiments, besides the fierce spirit of economic nationalism that was a crucial element in the freedom movement, and partly because the government has ineptly countered it. The controversy has caused the most fury in the agricultural sector. The anti-GATT campaign has been joined by several influential non-governmental organisations

(NGOs), as well as quasi-militant farmers' movements. The Karnataka Rajya Ryota Sangha (Karnataka State Farmers' Organisation), led by Professor M. D. Nanjundaswamy, unleashed a protest against Cargill India, a subsidiary of the US multinational Cargill Inc., and in December 1993 even set fire to its office near Bangalore, India's technological capital, because it was allegedly buying seeds cheaply from Indian farmers and reselling them at higher prices. The militant Hindi-belt farm leader Mahendra Singh Tikait of the Bharatiya Kisan Union (Indian Farmers' Union) has demanded a referendum on the GATT agreements.

The pace of economic reform is also impeded by the popular fear of the multinational corporations (MNCs). In 1993, 80 prominent citizens wrote to Prime Minister Rao, protesting the allotment of Kandla Port Trust land in Gujarat to Cargill South East Asia Ltd for making salt. Cargill was finally forced to withdraw from the project. On 3 March 1993, over 70 NGOs rallied in New Delhi, warning the government not to sign GATT while the BJP launched a nationwide anti-GATT movement in April 1994. A sign of the changing times, however, is the split in the farmers' movement with the more businesslike farmers, led by former bureaucrat Sharad Joshi's Shetkari Sangathana (Farmer's Organisation), coming out strongly in support of GATT, hoping to make gains from agricultural exports under the new trade regime.

To consolidate economic gains and to use them as a strength in electoral politics, the government needs to increase investment in the infrastructure. Other benefits, such as a rise in incomes and employment generation, must become visible soon. While organised sector employment for the second annual plans (1990–92) of the Five Year Plan increased by 1.6%, the number of registered job seekers grew by 5.2%; while the population increased by 2.03% in 1991, employment increased by only 1.5%. There is also a need for clearer long-term planning in agriculture, which contributes one-third of the GDP and employs two-thirds of the workforce. Reducing farm subsidies while making farm inputs cheaper, and providing a better price for produce and yet containing inflation, seem insurmountable challenges. But the political implications of agricultural economics cannot be ignored. Similarly, there is a need to watch for growing interstate disparities and fresh regional imbalances. These could have a destabilising effect at a time when investment will be concentrated in a few richer states with better infrastructure and political stability, threatening to turn large parts of the country into relatively backward suppliers of cheap manpower.

Militant environmentalism is a further source of friction, with several powerful NGOs opposing major development projects, as well as the harsher liberalisation measures. The most prominent are groups trying to obstruct the building of the Narmada Dam in the west-central states of Gujarat, Madhya Pradesh and Maharashtra. On three occasions the leaders of the movement threatened to drown themselves in the reservoir if work on the dam was not stopped. Similar protests have bedevilled major projects such as the Konkan Railway on the western coast, the east-coast highway and the Tehri Dam on the Ganga in the Uttar Pradesh Himalayas. The state and the activists have grown increasingly impatient with each other, resulting in a vicious cycle of militancy and repression.

Overall, reform risks being hamstrung by pressures on political stability, the persistence of abject poverty, and challenges of ethnic and regional tensions. Although India has already begun to feel, and enjoy, the geopolitical benefits of its economic change, long-term prospects for stability depend on astute management of reform, which has to take into account the fragility of the polity and society.

The Implications Of Economic Change

During his visit to Washington and meeting with US President Bill Clinton in June 1994, Prime Minister Rao emphasised the new presence that economic reform has given to India. He succeeded, at least temporarily, in shifting the focus of the India–US relationship to economic issues and away from contentious areas such as human rights and nuclear proliferation. The US visit was a high point in the new economically driven Indian diplomacy and Rao took the same 'we are open for business' message to other major Western capitals, including London, Bonn and Paris. The excitement about India as an emerging business and investment destination gave India an unexpected sense of power, which has not gone unnoticed within the region. At Geneva in March 1994, India's successful bid to block a Pakistani resolution on its human-rights record in Kashmir was widely ascribed (even by Pakistani analysts) to the strength that the size of its market gives India. Indian policy-makers, particularly Rao, have stated enthusiastically that they expect business prospects to shape the way the world relates to India in the future. The renaming of the Aid India Consortium as the India Development Forum is also significant.[9]

While India's relationship with the West is improving, the success of economic reform will determine India's ability to build long-term ties. On political issues, India's dealings with the US, for example, are bound to be stormy in the short term. But it is reasonable to assume that Washington would view India differently if the trade between the two countries increased from the current $7.5bn. It is still too early to expect India to acquire the same importance as China in trade terms. But if trade reached $15bn and direct US investments grew in the next three years, which is not impossible, the equation would change. India has actively encouraged the setting up of an India Interest Group consisting of 31 major US multinational corporations investing in India, and this has become a useful lobby. Within the region a shift in popular and political focus towards economics might help to revive the South Asian Association for Regional Cooperation (SAARC) as a trading bloc. As SAARC has so far failed to be an effective body and could continue to be dogged by the smaller nations' insecurities about an enormous India, New Delhi has been exploring other trading blocs in the region. There is some interest in the proposal for an Indian Ocean economic bloc put forward by former South African Foreign Minister R. F. Botha on his visit to New Delhi in November 1993.

Economic change is also creating a new class of people in power, while rebuilding the corrupt order that thrived on the licence-quota raj. Traditionally, in the Indian mind 'capitalist' was a pejorative term commonly translated as 'profiteer' or 'exploiter'. Bureaucrats as well as political leaders kept their distance from industrialists in public, even as many of them accepted liberal bribes. Only in the past two years has a Prime Minister begun to invite captains of industry and chambers of commerce officials on foreign visits with him. Corruption is still considerable, but the vast and complicated nexus of patronage and bribery involving bureaucrats, businessmen and politicians is under strain. While it is true that reform itself has produced scandals, notably the 1992 Rs2bn share-market scam and the massive sugar import disgrace in 1994, at least the institutionalised corruption based on industrial licensing is on its way out.[10]

In terms of internal politics, economic change has already had positive results. The widespread enthusiasm for stock-market investments among the middle classes is creating a vested interest in peace and financial security that transcends ethnic, linguistic and communal boundaries. In March 1993, the Bombay Stock Exchange, India's premier money-market, resumed trading within 24 hours of the serial bombings that claimed 348 lives – 46 of them in the blast at the stock-exchange building. As private enterprise burgeons, the urban middle classes look like being given a stake in industrial peace and law and order.[11] This is important as economic reform has to move simultaneously with the growth of communalism, casteism and secessionism. The crucial question is, which will be the stronger: the positive forces generated domestically and internationally by economic change; or the negative ones unleashed by violent movements of various kinds? Already the rout of the Congress in three of the four states that went to the polls in November–December 1994 was being viewed as a call for a halt to the Party's drive towards economic reform.

Internal Politics
Such sweeping economic change is being carried out in a splintered society. The forces of casteism and communalism have become much more threatening than previously and, with persistent secessionist movements, form a kind of trident at the heart of India's secular constitutional polity. This has been accentuated by certain developments in domestic politics since 1989 and the timing of several negative changes. Unlike the secessionist movements in the past, the two most recent ones, by Sikhs in Punjab and Muslims in the Kashmir valley, have clear religious links. Hindu revivalist parties, notably the BJP, have thus been able to exploit insecurities among the majority community. Hitherto, secessionist movements in the tribal north-eastern states were seen primarily as ethnic and regional, although there were some allegations of the involvement of the church and foreign pastors. The Dravida movement in the southern state of Tamil Nadu in the 1960s was actually anti-religion, a partly atheist backlash against Brahmanical domination.

But rebellions in Punjab and the Kashmir valley, seen as being controlled from the respective shrines of the Sikhs and the Muslims, strengthened the BJP's old argument that Hindus were the only real nationalists with a genuine stake in India. This helped the forces of Hindu communalism to coalesce around the symbolic issue of the destruction of the medieval mosque in Ayodhya, the birthplace of Lord Ram, and the 'reconstruction' there of the temple that Mir Baqi, the General of Babur, founder of the Mughal dynasty, was said to have destroyed in the sixteenth century. Hindu revival, however, was seen by the multitudes of lower castes as primarily an upper-caste movement. At the same time, it caused communal riots and made Muslims more insecure. As a consequence, both groups, the Congress Party's trusted and vital vote banks, were alienated. Communal politics in the Hindi heartland (which contributes more than half the seats to Lok Sabha), led to a flow of Hindu votes towards the BJP, and the Party scored major successes in the two elections of

1989 and 1991.[12] This exacerbated the alienation of the lower castes and Muslims, who no longer saw Congress as a dominant party that could provide security and promote the move towards equality. Unwilling to vote for a losing party, they came together in a new electoral alliance that achieved unprecedented successes and is now ruling India's most populous and politically significant state of Uttar Pradesh (which contributes 85 seats, or 15% of members, to the Lok Sabha). Such polarisation was completely unfamiliar to the political pundits in India; it punched gaping holes in the old Congress umbrella under which the minorities and 'weaker sections' (the large mass of backward classes and lower-castes) traditionally sought refuge.

The result is new caste tension. And because it has overlapped with a sharp increase in communal violence, following the destruction of the mosque in Ayodhya by Hindu fundamentalists, the emergence of Muslim militancy and growing secessionist pressures, it has left the state machinery fatigued and impatient. The state has tended to use a disproportionate amount of force, giving great freedom to overused and harassed paramilitary and police forces. Dealing with such cycles of civil strife, repression and increased alienation are traditionally part of the job of governing India, but the new factor is that the threat to constitutional polity comes not merely from the familiar, minority-led secessionist movements, but also from the political, economic and social mainstream of the nation.

A Majority's Minority Complex

The vital concern in domestic politics is the Hindu–Muslim divide at its centre. So far, Indian politics has been clearly polarised: Congress on the one side, and the rest of the opposition uniting on the other. To be with or against the Congress was the main item on the national political agenda, particularly after the mid-1970s when Congress began to veer away from socialism and lost even the support of the pro-Moscow communist factions. This led to several alliances among non-Congress parties, including occasions when the BJP and the Left arrived at electoral understandings. A shared hatred of Congress transcended ideological barriers, but now, with the BJP's swerve to the right, this has changed.

The roots of India's communal tensions are demographic and historical, as well as political. Notionally, Hindus constitute 82% of India's population, Muslims around 12% and the remainder comprises Sikhs, Christians and tiny minorities of Buddhists, Parsis (Zoroastrians) and Jews. But the figure for the Hindus is a census fallacy: it includes a large number of tribal sects, many of whom are animists or neo-Hindus. There are also numerous subdivisions of caste, ethnicity and language among the Hindus. The growth of the currently active fundamentalist parties, however, is linked to the history of the freedom movement and the 1947 Partition of the subcontinent.[13] The national volunteer corps Rashtriya Swayam-sevak Sangh (RSS), which is now the most important Hindu revival-ist organisation, was set up in 1924. K. B. Hedgewar, a founding father, gave it an activist shape, combining physical exercise and military organisation with revivalist ideology.

The RSS emerged as one of the saviours of the Hindus during Hindu–Muslim riots triggered by the Partition. But it was soon under pressure as Nathu Ram Godse, Mahatma Gandhi's assassin, was alleged to have had links with it. The government imposed a ban on the RSS in 1948, which lasted two years. In the following years, the RSS and other Hindu revivalist groups found several campaign causes, the first being opposition to the Hindu Code Bill that aimed to codify and reform traditional Hindu personal law, and which had been a subject of detailed discussion in the Rajya Sabha (the Upper House of Parliament) in 1952.[14] The revivalists demanded a common personal law for all Indians, irrespective of religion, and called the legislation 'pseudo-secular'. This was followed in the mid-1960s by a nationwide movement to ban cow slaughter.

To coordinate their efforts, mainly to oppose Christian proselytis-ing, in April 1964 the Hindu organisations also created the umbrella group Vishwa Hindu Parishad (VHP, or the World Hindu Council). Now this group is leading the Ayodhya campaign. Also, by the 1960s, the Bharatiya Jana Sangh (BJS), founded in 1951, emerged as the political front of the RSS.[15] Later it grew into a strong political party, less doctrinaire than the RSS, but relying on it for ideological and physical sustenance. Its leadership, although mostly drawn from RSS ranks, has tried to veer towards the centre. This is also true of the BJP, the latest incarnation of the Jana Sangh.

Why have these parties succeeded in suddenly increasing their following so substantially, when the broad thrust of the socio-eco-nomic and cultural movement of Indian society should have been towards greater integration? This has happened at a time when the Muslim community was showing signs of renewed confidence and increased participation in mainstream areas of business and politics and when modern and nationalistic Muslim role-models were ap-pearing in fields ranging from science to sports, politics to soldiery, and business to art and cinema.

Behind this lies the paradox of a majority acquiring a minority complex. The traditional view is that Hindus feel threatened and isolated because the rest of the world is non-Hindu. There is a dominant Christian world and a large Islamic world, but since Hindus are primarily confined to India, how can Hindu nationalism not be synonymous with Indian nationalism? Politically, the BJP and its several earlier avatars have tried to fuel this with the charge of 'minorityism' against the Congress and other dominant centrist parties. The minorities (i.e., Muslims), the charge goes, are being appeased at the cost of the Hindus just because they vote *en bloc* in elections. Other grievances are that the government gives special status to minority cultural and educational institutions to prevent integration, while Hindus are suffering a dilution of their religious beliefs and practices because of a liberalisation that spares other religions. Among the list of complaints are: that Hindus are the only community to have accepted family planning (so while their numbers are diminishing, those of the Muslims are increasing); Hindu religious institutions are starved of funds while Muslims and Christians get foreign money; and, most dangerous of all, that if there was ever a justification for a secular India it was taken away by Partition. The BJP has also tried to make a major issue of Jammu and Kashmir's special status, with autonomy under Article 370 of the Constitution, 'just because it has a Muslim majority'. The central argument has been that if Muslims demanded the Partition of the country in 1947 and now have special status in the only state where they are in a majority, how can they be patriotic Indians?[16]

The BJP benefited in the mid-1980s from several politically expedient concessions made by Rajiv Gandhi to the Muslim clergy that ran contrary to the spirit of secularism and were seen as blatant examples of minorityism. These included the alacrity with which India banned Salman Rushdie's *Satanic Verses* and bent over backwards, in what came to be known as the Shah Bano case, to appease the Muslim clergy on the constitutional question of whether or not the nation's secular courts could intervene to provide divorced Muslim women with maintenance from their husbands.[17]

Thus the Hindu groups, who draw strength mainly from the community's resentment over centuries of subjugation by Muslim invaders and from an ancient fear of militant Islam, were given an axe to grind. It was these historical hatreds and now 'irrefutable' evidence of minority appeasement that created, from the BJP's point of view, an auspicious set of circumstances to exploit the issue of the Ram Janmabhoomi in Ayodhya. Here, Hindu anger was provoked by the belief that if the medieval Muslim invaders made it their business to raze Hindu temples to the ground and build mosques in their place, modern-day Hindus should be permitted to restore what they consider one of their most hallowed shrines.

The Afghan *jihad*, the Iranian revolution, increasing fundamentalist fervour in Pakistan despite the religious parties' defeat in the 1993 elections, the Islamic resurgence in Central Asia, and now the Islamic militancy in Kashmir, have deepened Hindu anxiety. It is no surprise that the BJP was so successful in elections between November 1989 and February 1990.

The future will be determined by the way the BJP is able to sort out the confusions and contradictions that dog its world view. The founders of the RSS claimed that their aim was not to acquire political power. Yet the organisation and the political party it created have steadfastly worked towards that single objective. The RSS was set up as a cultural and ideological organisation to secure the domination of the Hindus, and yet BJP leaders, including its current president L. K. Advani, have been at pains to claim that they believe in a secular constitution, but that only they could give India 'real' secularism. Today, on the one hand the Party talks of Ram Rajya (a reign akin to the pristine example set by Lord Ram in Ayodhya), while on the other it argues that the concept is not religious. In its statement on national issues on the eve of the elections to five provincial assemblies in November 1993, the Party described Ram Rajya as being 'rooted in the collective memory of people, which epitomises the quest for happiness and glory of the Indian people'.[18] This formula was contrived to meet secular electoral requirements to avoid defining Ram Rajya as a specifically Hindu concept – and it left the voters rather confused. The November poll saw a clear rebuff to the BJP, which had triumphantly approached it as a referendum on its ideology, but ended up with embarrassing reverses. The lesson to the Party, which had promised to build a temple where the mosque stood earlier, was clear: building a shrine does not have the same romance as destroying one. But BJP mandarins saw great hope in the Party's creditable performance in the Karnataka assembly elections in December 1994, where it won 40 seats compared to four in 1989. In fact, began its new campaign using *swadeshi* (self-reliance) not Ram, as its linchpin, with a protest against the economic reforms by the Swadeshi Jagran Manch in Patna on 30 November 1994.

Predictably, the electoral disaster has caused anxiety. For the moment, the relative centrists seem to have the upper hand as the Party worries about the growing numbers of very poor, and wrestles with the lower-caste alliance that cut into its Hindu votes. There are demands from cautious groups within the Party to alter its *chehra, chaal, charitra* (face, direction, character). Proponents of social engineering, such as the ideologue K. Govindacharya, are pushing for a clear strategy to win lower- and intermediate-caste votes rather than a long-term plan to unite the Hindu community. Govindacharya, himself from the lower castes, has been given a higher profile in the Party, as has the female MP Uma Bharati, illustrating the BJP's quest for political correctness. Overall, in a blatant strategy to deal with new caste equations, the Party is bringing lower castes into the forefront, thus attenuating its original philosophy of uniting through (Hindu) culture what (Hindu society) has been divided by caste. How the BJP remoulds itself will have policy implications across the board.

With the BJP finally realising that the temple issue, electorally, is akin to a cheque they have already cashed, it is reasonable to predict that xenophobia will be an essential component of their new strategy. This could limit New Delhi's freedom of action in the foreign policy field. With India trying to globalise its economy, this will encompass both the foreign and economic policies.

The BJP campaign could be built around allegations of the surrender of economic sovereignty and nuclear plans to the West, the signing of GATT, and anything else that appears a concession to Pakistan. Other strands could be the fear of pan-Islamic fundamentalism, continuing concern about the immigration of predominantly Muslim migrant labour from Bangladesh, and long-term defence and nuclear policies. The BJP is the only major party to have publicly, and in election manifestos, promised a nuclearised weapons programme. How much of it is to serve a jingoistic constituency and how much will be translated into policy and action if the Party came to power is academic. The two occasions in the past when the BJP shared power, directly or indirectly (in the 1977 Janata Party and while supporting V. P. Singh's Janata Dal from outside in 1989), it did not embarrass its coalition partners by demanding changes in nuclear policy. In opposition the BJP can influence these policies more as it is not constrained by the responsibilities of leadership.

The BJP's economic campaign is likely to be caught in its own contradiction – traditional adherence to market-oriented capitalism, and the narrow political need to raise xenophobic anxiety. Through decades of socialism, the Party fought for a free economy, but when the Rao government began doing much the same thing, the Party found its main political rival taking away its strongest unique selling proposition. Hence it took up a fiercely nationalistic and inward-looking posture. At present, BJP thought on the economy is split in three directions. One extreme is led by former Party president Murli Manohar Joshi, who foresees in the rapid consumerisation of Indian society deleterious Westernisation and MNC domination. The other extreme, represented by MP Jaswant Singh, has been assuring the chambers of commerce that they have nothing to fear from the BJP in power. Perched in the middle is BJP president L. K. Advani who declared that his party was for liberalisation, but against globalisation.[19] But the BJP's alternative budget for 1994–95 shows that its economic policy vision is fundamentally the same as that of Rao's Congress. The BJP would probably try to have the best of both worlds, vigorously talking of the free economy but limiting liberalisation to domestic markets, while retaining barriers between India and the world. That is why the Party has transmuted its opposition to reform into a *swadeshi* movement.

It is unlikely, however, that if voted to power the BJP would make a serious effort to translate its rhetoric into policy, whether it is an aggressive, anti-Islamic world approach, the determination to push back '15 million' illegal immigrants from Bangladesh, or even the threat to withdraw from GATT. Fundamentally, the Party is still pro-business and pro-trader, as was evident when the newly elected BJP state government in Delhi, in its most significant decision so far, slashed the sales tax in the capital after coming to power in December 1993. The Party has to resolve a persistent dilemma: if it adheres to the stridently right-wing Hindu platform it cannot widen its support, and if it moves towards the centre, it tends to make itself indistinguishable from other parties, thus alienating its loyalists. There are two clear long-term aspects to the growth of the BJP and Hindu revivalism. First, irrespective of the BJP's electoral fortunes, Hindu revivalism would cast its shadow over domestic, economic, international and security policies. Second, it would bring enormous additional pressures to a state already wrestling with several ethno-linguistic or religious separatist movements. It is one thing when a distant, tribal minority, such as the Nagas, campaigns for secession, or even a prominent minority, such as the Sikhs, is in revolt. It is quite another when the dominant majority also begins to question the constitutional polity, in which independent India offers statutory security and equal coexistence to its minorities. Even if the voters keep the BJP out of power, the Party will continue to influence the national agenda. This will present the relatively secular parties with a difficult choice. If they achieve a *modus vivendi* with the BJP, it will amount to appeasement. If they meet the Hindu nationalists head on, it will lead to confrontation – which is just what the BJP needs to revive its fortunes. It is likely, however, that Rao and his successors would persist with the present policy of calculated opposition to the BJP while conceding to some of the more reasonable demands of the Hindus.

The Caste Factor

The BJP phenomenon has affected stability by exacerbating the caste factor, thus fracturing the Hindu vote. Caste has been a crucial issue in all political calculations, particularly during elections, but it began to acquire an entirely new dimension in 1990 when the then ruling party, Janata Dal, under Prime Minister V. P. Singh, embarked on an electoral policy that cynically exploited caste. The government announced the implementation of the decade-old Mandal Commission report, which recommended that 25% of all government jobs be reserved for members of the intermediate castes, or Other Backward Classes (OBCs). The Indian Constitution already follows an affirmative-action policy under which 28% of all jobs are reserved for scheduled castes (former untouchables) and tribals. The implementation of the Mandal Commission recommendations took more than 50% of government jobs out of the reach of the upper castes. The ensuing upper-caste revolt paralysed the government and led, in autumn 1990, to a violent public protest, as 159 young upper-caste students attempted to burn themselves and 63 died. This ultimately contributed to the fall of the government, but by then caste had become a central concern.

Another decisive turn in caste politics came as a breakaway group of Singh's party and the Bahujan Samaj Party (BSP, a new party of the scheduled castes), formed a lower-caste–Muslim alliance that won power in the crucial state of Uttar Pradesh. The rise of the BSP has significant policy implications. It is led by the mercurial Kanshi Ram, a former scientist at the Defence Ministry's explosives research laboratory at Pune, who became a political leader of national standing through the familiar route of trade unionism. Given his education and white-collar background, it was expected that once he came to power in a state he would follow the trend established by other ideological or sectarian parties and modify his policies. But hopes were short-lived as his deputy, Mayawati, publicly denounced Mahatma Gandhi as an upper-caste bigot. For Hindu fundamentalists, the situation has elements of alarming *déjà vu*. They see it as a dangerous inroad by chronic conspirators determined to destroy the cohesion of Hindu society.

A further effect of caste and religious politics, particularly in the Hindi heartland, is the prospect of an even weaker Centre. The Rao government is the first in nearly five years to have a majority, albeit a thin one, of its own. But it is difficult to tell whether power at the Centre can be sustained or even enhanced. The Congress Party's old vote banks in the Hindi heartland have been swept away by caste and communalism. In the south, it is unable to break the stranglehold of the regional All India Anna Dravida Munnetra Kazhagam (AIADMK) in the large state of Tamil Nadu, while the Left still has considerable influence in Kerala. In the other large southern state of Andhra Pradesh, the regional Telugu Desam Party (TDP) swept to power with 219 out of 294 seats in the assembly elections in December 1994. In Karnataka, too, the Congress was voted out of the assembly when the number of seats it won fell from 176 to 35 in a 224-member house in the December elections.

Political uncertainties were also highlighted by the vicious dissidence that rocked the Congress Party immediately after it was routed in the provincial assembly elections in Karnataka and Andhra Pradesh. Led by Human Resources Development Minister Arjun Singh (Rao's main rival for the premiership), the dissidents produced a formidable charter of demands that included putting a 'human face to economic reform'. Singh was joined by N. D. Tiwari, Congress leader from the Hindi-speaking political heartland, and they based their campaign on a veiled criticism of the Rao government's reform and other policies. These fissures in the Congress Party and the dip in its electoral fortunes, with the simultaneous rise in the power of the regional parties, have significant long-term consequences, effectively extinguishing the Congress Party's hopes of acquiring large majorities at the Centre in the future.

The splintering of the Hindi-heartland vote means that unless there are upheavals, India is in for a long spell of coalition politics. And although it could be argued that historically a strong Centre, particularly under Indira and Rajiv Gandhi, has worked to India's detriment, destroying the federal spirit of the Constitution and depriving states of their legitimate constitutional powers, on the other hand, weaker, coalition-based central governments have resulted in instability, indecision and a lack of direction at policy-making levels. Thus the prospect of a diminished Centre is fraught with uncertainties, particularly as fragmentary and centrifugal forces are still evident in many regions of the country.

II. THE SEPARATIST THREAT

It is an old adage that only cricket or war can unite the people of India. The stereotypes are well known: the perennial Hindu–Muslim communal divide; the unrest in Punjab and Kashmir; tribal separatism in north-east India; the occasional and considerably restrained Hindu–Christian rivalries in some parts of the country; and friction between followers of the same faith (e.g., caste problems among the Hindus, Shia–Sunni clashes among the Muslims and vicious differences between puritanical Sikhs and adherents of the Radha Soami and Nirankari sects). It is impossible to put sociological labels on such conflicts, given the complicated and often contradictory meshing of the underlying factors. People fight over ethnicity, religion, language, caste, political autonomy, economic disparities and often over a combination of these.

Conflicts that seem completely religious or political on the surface in India usually have an ethnic, linguistic or regional dimension. In the past, the southern state of Tamil Nadu saw a strong Dravid ethnic movement that resulted in the transfer of political power from Congress, seen to be dominated by the Brahmins, to the non-Brahmin, regional Dravida Munnetra Kazhagam (DMK) party. This Party, or its offshoots, has ruled the state for nearly two decades. In the neighbouring Andhra Pradesh, ageing star of Telugu-language cinema N. T. Rama Rao brought his Telugu Desam Party to the forefront by exploiting Telugu pride. The Gorkha demand for autonomy in the hill district of Darjeeling in West Bengal was at least temporarily settled by the creation of an autonomous district council under the overall, but limited, control of the state government. In eastern and central India, a new ethnic movement for a separate state and political power is gathering momentum under the leadership of the Jharkhand Mukti Morcha (JMM, Jharkhand Liberation Front), an organisation of the most impoverished plains tribals of the states of Bihar, Orissa, West Bengal and Madhya Pradesh.

The Naga tribals fought for decades after Independence to preserve their ethnicity, which they felt was threatened by 'Indianisation'; but they also fought to preserve their Christianity which they saw, however erroneously, as being threatened by an influx of Hindus from the plains. And they fought for political autonomy and for a right to be heard – a matter of serious concern for a distinct ethnic community that forms no more than 0.15% of a massive national population. The Assamese, who engaged in eight years of agitation against the illegal migration of Bangladeshis into their tea-

and oil-rich state, were defending their ethnicity, language, political power and religion in an area where they were outnumbered by Bengali-speaking Muslim immigrants. The same mixture of religious, ethnic and political tensions is true of the ongoing conflicts in Punjab and Kashmir.

Even tiny and seemingly ethnically 'clean' states, with populations of only a million or less, have to live with ethnic tensions. There is the Hynniewtrep movement in the north-eastern state of Meghalaya, which demands a separate state for the dominant Khasi and Jaintia tribes (while their ethnic cousins the Garos are left to fend for themselves); the demand by less than 100,000 Kukis of Manipur for a separate state of their own bordering Burma; and, occasionally, similar demands made by the Ao subtribe in Nagaland, and less than 50,000 Buddhist Chakmas who feel 'oppressed' by Mizoram's 500,000 Mizos. These are all states carved out fairly recently to provide self-governance to distinct tribal groups and with populations ranging between three-quarters of a million to two million. Yet none of these movements should be lightly dismissed: the Chakmas in Bangladeshi regions bordering India's Mizoram and Tripura states have been involved in insurgency for a decade, resulting in thousands of deaths. Clashes between the Kukis and the Naga tribes in Manipur in 1993 resulted in nearly 200 deaths and required army intervention.

These figures make India the most fractious democracy in the world. Before and after Independence, India has had an exceptional record of civil strife, often separatist, in one region or another. And yet it has not only survived, it has actually, if marginally, expanded in size, with the inclusion of the former protectorate of Sikkim in the Union. It has absorbed most of the separatist movements in its constitutional entity, just as, over centuries, most of the invasions in the subcontinent's north-west were absorbed into the mainstream of Indian society. India seems to have evolved a doctrine of its own to fight separatist movements, although whether it will be effective with the current conflicts, or those likely to emerge in future, is uncertain.

Lessons From The North-East
Independent India's first brush with separatism came in the predominantly tribal, mountainous, thickly-wooded and relatively inaccessible north-eastern region of the country bordering China, Burma and the former East Pakistan (now Bangladesh). It is here, fighting insurgencies by Naga, Mizo and Manipuri ethnic groups, besides a

24

smaller one by the tribals of Tripura, and the separatist fringes of the Assam movement against foreign infiltrators, that India developed its own method of countering separatism. Broadly, it is a three-step strategy: to fight the insurgency with military force for some time; then, when the rebellion seems to be tiring, offer negotiations; and finally, when the rebels are convinced that no matter what the casualties on either side, they are not going to be able to secede, win them over with the offer of constitutional sops, invariably resulting in power being given to them following an election. All this is done within the parameters of the Constitution, although often by amending it. There are legions of former underground 'generals' in several states where insurgency was endemic, who were sworn in as ministers or legislators on the Indian Constitution, and who now fly the Indian tricolour on their government cars or don armed police uniforms.[1]

India's initial efforts to crush insurgencies militarily are sobering. The Indian Army's approach paper to the Fourth National Pay Commission in 1984 stated that since Independence, the Army had lost nearly 40,000 men in various conflicts. Of these, less than 12,000 died in the four wars with Pakistan and China. Nearly 10,000 Indian soldiers died since the December 1971 Bangladesh War, the last international conflict in which India had been involved until then (the IPKF operations in Sri Lanka came four years later). Nearly three-quarters of all Army casualties resulted from involvement in fighting separatist domestic violence. At the peak of the insurgency, 13 Army brigades – many of them oversized – were deployed in the north-east. A school of counter-insurgency and jungle warfare was set up in Mizoram and a counter-insurgency corps headquarters was established in Dimapur, in the Naga foothills.

The central message of India's north-eastern experience is that if fought ruthlessly, rebellions run their natural course and, after peaking, are susceptible to negotiated settlements. The insurgency in Nagaland was the bloodiest and lasted the longest (nearly three decades), but in 1975 the dominant underground faction signed what is known as the Shillong Peace Agreement under which a separate state had been carved out for the Naga tribe and with the promise of constitutional safeguards – cultural, ethnic, political as well as economic. The Nagas, who began guerrilla warfare in the mid-1950s, were finally convinced that they were unlikely to achieve independence in the face of a determined state and its army. When they decided to settle, New Delhi showed remarkable sophistication in answering their concerns: the new state was given special status under the Constitution, outsiders were forbidden to take up jobs or buy property there, and a subclause was added to the Constitution giving Nagas exclusive ownership of mineral resources in the region.

Similarly, in Mizoram the leader of the underground Mizo National Front (MNF), Laldenga, was persuaded by two decades of bloodshed that even if he and the core of his followers survived the bush war they would not achieve sovereignty. A decade after the Naga accord, the Mizos too developed elaborate excuses to convince their followers that this was not capitulation. Their justification for settling was that there was no point in fighting when reasonable freedom was available within India, and suggesting that if sovereignty by itself meant freedom, then surely Poland would be a truly free country.[2] The MNF moved overground following an accord signed in 1985, was elected to power in the election held specially under the accord, and was roundly defeated in the subsequent elections, completing the process of its absorption into India's constitutional mainstream. New Delhi had again succeeded with the strategy first tried in Nagaland.

The movement in Assam presented a different challenge as it was predominantly peaceful and non-secessionist and yet had a sizeable, violent and separatist fringe. This popular mass movement against the infiltration of Bangladeshi migrants crippled the state's economy, stopped the flow of crude oil and impeded the supplies of tea and plywood to inland markets (Assam produces 70% of India's on-shore oil and the bulk of its tea), and resulted in nearly 8,000 deaths between 1978 and 1983. But New Delhi had begun to distil lessons from its experience in the region and a modified version of the same three-stage strategy was employed. There was brutal suppression accompanied by protracted negotiations. In 1985, the Congress (I) government, which came to power in a forced, farcical election in 1983, was dismissed, and fresh elections were held under an accord with the Central government led by Rajiv Gandhi and his Congress (I). This accord also promised constitutional safeguards to answer the ethnic, linguistic and political insecurities of the Assamese. As in Mizoram, in Assam the elections held under the accord swept the agitators to power as the Asom Gana Parishad (AGP), but they were only to be thrown out in the following elections. The AGP is now disparate and faction-ridden, a Congress (I) government is in power, and although the popular disenchantment with corrupt politics has resulted in the appearance of some militant groups, the overall picture is much brighter than a decade ago.

Broadly, these are instances of the political and constitutional system being able to accommodate separatist movements after a long period of unrelenting softening through military pressure. This was done either by sharing power, by creating new ethno-political territories or by making minor political concessions. These included, for example, giving the tribes the legal right to their mineral resources and offering protection, such as requiring inner-line entry permits and prohibiting outsiders from buying properties in tribal regions. Even while fighting violent insurgencies, the state was not shy of continuing a dialogue with the rebel. A great deal of sophistication was employed in structuring the peace process and agreements: the rebels did not 'surrender weapons' to the government, they 'handed them over' to be kept in safehouses, sometimes supervised by a peace council consisting mainly of tribal elders. They did not 'surrender', they 'abjured violence'. That the state scrupulously avoided claims of victory and the underground did not have to admit defeat are key elements of the strategy.[3]

Why Kashmir And Punjab Are Different
The future of India's policies and prospects for stability will depend on whether it can use a similar, if modified, doctrine to tackle its two current problems: Punjab and Kashmir. Here, as in the north-east, the separatist campaigns feed on a minority's sense of alienation. There is a degree of popular support (considerably more in the Kashmir valley than in Punjab), and clear foreign backing with continuous arms supplies, as in the north-east. But there are also vital differences:

- None of the Naga, Mizo and Manipuri rebels were driven by religious fervour, which was certainly the case with Sikh militancy and is, today, the dominant factor in the Kashmir valley. In the north-east, the church actually aided mediation efforts and helped to work towards peace; whereas Kashmir attracts pan-Islamic interest and, in Punjab, the holiest Sikh shrines became the spiritual, temporal and operational centres of the militancy.

- Unlike in Punjab, none of the tribal rebellions involved frontline Indian communities. In the mind of the average Indian, rebellion in the north-east was a distant blur, but Punjab and Kashmir are close to the country's northern political hub. Even when it came to reconciliation, there was no adverse reaction when constitutional sops were given to the north-eastern tribes, but any visible concessions made to Sikh or Kashmiri militants are bound to have political repercussions.

- It was easier to localise the rebellions in the north-east. Each one was seen as a local battle between a tribe and the Indian state. Punjab and Kashmir involve the interests of the large national majority, as in both the states the Hindu minority is seen as the sufferer. Every terrorist incident involving killings or damage to the Hindus in these states provokes nationwide outrage.

- Times have changed. With the development of national and international media, modern communications and the worldwide focus on human rights, it is increasingly difficult to execute the first repressive phase of the strategy without inviting international opprobrium. Satellite TV spreads images of incidents, such as the destruction of the Ayodhya shrine, the siege of Hazratbal mosque in Kashmir or human-rights abuses – it is impossible for India to hide a part of its territory or its people from the world.

The factors that made Punjab so different from the north-eastern insurgencies, and prohibited the old crush–tear–accommodate strategy, ultimately became the key to solving the problem, at least in the short term. A Punjabi-dominated army found it difficult to operate in Punjab – it suffered enormous damage from a rash of mutinies following its assault on the Golden Temple in June 1984. The government was thus forced into handing over counter-insurgency operations to the Punjab police. For the first time in the long history of counter-insurgency in India, the local police, consisting mainly of Sikhs, carried out raids, ambushes and road-checks while the Army confined itself to a secondary role, such as providing cordon security during search operations. A high-profile and ruthless Sikh director-general succeeded in turning Punjab into a Sikh versus Sikh battle with his police ranged against the militants, who did not help their cause by massacring the policemen's families.

The Sikh policemen knew the terrain, had their own contacts within the rural population and, most significantly, were not seen as an instrument of an oppressive anti-Sikh government in New Delhi. Several other factors contributed, such as the use of innovative tactics that toed the fine line between what is legal or legitimate and what is not, and often transgressed it. The militant tactic of kidnapping police officers' families was answered with counter-kidnappings and subsequent exchanges. Large cash rewards were offered for key militants, and informants were given new identities in distant parts of the country to escape retribution. Extrajudicial killings and arrests were freely condoned. The construction of an expensive security fence along the border also helped to check the movement of arms from Pakistan and the flight of the militants to sanctuaries there. Ultimately the militants contributed to the success of these tactics by criminalising their own movement, indulging in extortion, rape and reckless vendetta killings. If the government succeeded in turning the local police against the militants, the militants managed to turn most of the population against themselves, and that signalled a decline in the violence, as the decreasing number of killings in the state testifies.[4]

The respite, however, could be temporary as many of the major politico-economic factors underlying the trouble persist. The Sikh religious party, the Shiromani Akali Dal, now split into several factions, still has a large following. It was because of factionalism that the party was not able to translate its support into state assembly seats in the general elections of 1992 and in the subsequent by-elections. It is a tradition in Punjab that when in power the Akalis are patriotic nationalists, and once out of power they begin to talk of Khalistan, or a sovereign theocratic Sikh state. That is precisely what happened at the end of May 1994. If they were to regroup, patronise a separatist agenda and succeed in making the gurudwaras (Sikh temples) their pulpit again, it could revive Sikh unrest and ultimately militancy.

Unable to depart from the familiar pattern in Indian politics, the Rao government has failed to exploit the tactical gains on the north-eastern pattern. In Punjab, this would have meant returning the Akalis to power, which would have marked a real homecoming for the middle-ground Sikh politicians. Instead, an effort has been made to strengthen the state's Congress government, consigning Akali politics to a firm adversarial role. Again, consistent with the north-eastern formula, the ideal time for the Centre to make political gestures to assuage the Sikhs was when militancy was on the decline. It is in this procrastination, a dangerous 'out of sight, out of mind' approach towards what was until recently India's foremost problem, that the seeds of a militant revival in Punjab could lie. To consign its greatest internal threat firmly to history India would be wise to remember the most important lesson of its north-eastern doctrine: there can be no lasting peace if the warring groups are not eased into the political mainstream.

The Kashmir Issue
Unlike any other separatist movement in India, Kashmir has an international dimension. Many Western powers, particularly the US, consider it to be disputed territory and that Pakistan has the right to interfere (at least politically and diplomatically) while claiming that

it has no role in fomenting or supporting insurgency. The West, and again particularly the US, links the Kashmir issue to their nuclear concerns in the region: Kashmir is a likely and dangerous *casus belli* between India and Pakistan, and as both antagonists are nuclear-capable, the war could end with the losing side using weapons of mass destruction as a last desperate measure. The two other elements of international interest are human rights and Islam. In the post-Cold War world, human rights has not only moved up the international agenda, it has also been depoliticised to the extent that it is no longer a stick with which to beat the Eastern or communist bloc. India's cause has not been helped by the unrestrained behaviour of its security forces, particularly the paramilitary forces that used excessive firepower and brute intimidation against the Valley Muslims. This was a result of mechanically employing the north-eastern approach without adjusting to the unique demands of the situation, partly caused by the attitude that the Kashmiri Muslims have never been loyal Indians and are a large Pakistani fifth-column anyway.

Arguing that the Kashmiri rebellion is led entirely by the Valley Muslims, Pakistan has also succeeded in putting the issue on the agenda of the Organisation of Islamic Countries (OIC), while giving it a pan-Islamic character involving international Islamic NGOs on the one hand, and on the other the leftover but dangerously armed rabble of the Afghan war. As more and more Afghan veterans (including Arabs of various nationalities), fighting for money, religious commitment or both, were killed or captured by Indian security forces in 1994, a new tactical and political dimension is being added to the crisis in a region bordering Pakistan and China, and close geographically and ethno-religiously to Central Asia.

The outline of an Indian policy to contain this threat is now visible. Its core is still the north-eastern doctrine; although insurgency will be fought with much greater restraint by the security forces to avoid incidents of human-rights abuse. At the same time, there is an effort to split the rebellion along two lines: the relatively secular, independence-seeking Jammu and Kashmir Liberation Front (JKLF); and the fundamentalist, pro-Pakistan groups spearheaded by the Hizb ul Mujahedin. New Delhi has, time and again, shown willingness to talk to the JKLF and Pakistan has responded by isolating the group and weakening it by denying it weaponry and other aid while strengthening the fundamentalist groups seeking to merge with Pakistan.

New Delhi's long-term policy is to initiate some kind of a political process in the state where elections have not been held for seven years. Ideally, the election could follow an accord with the JKLF and middle-ground groups such as the Jammu and Kashmir Hurriyat (Independence) Conference, an apex organisation of several disparate political, religious and social groups. If that is not possible, New Delhi might try to hold an election by supporting former Chief Minister Farooq Abdullah and his National Conference Party. Although he is the son of former Kashmiri stalwart Sheikh Abdullah, Farooq Abdullah is now seen by the Valley Muslims as a betrayer of the Kashmiri cause. A better solution could be to restore to the state the kind of autonomy promised in 1948 under Article 370 of the Constitution; this was put into effect in 1952, only to be eroded slowly in the next four decades. But here the Centre is severely constrained by domestic politics: the BJP has already made the withdrawal of Article 370 a vital election plank, and any measure seen as giving a region special status merely because of its Muslim majority will add fuel to the Party's 'Muslims are being appeased' campaign. The longer New Delhi denies Kashmiris constitutional autonomy, the more distant a long-term solution will become. If it concedes autonomy, it may offer the BJP, now down on its luck, just the cause it needs to revive its electoral fortunes.

It is because of these complications that the likely medium-term prognosis for Kashmir is continuing drift and violence. Pakistan will use the combination of international, regional and domestic factors as a chance to 'settle' the Kashmir issue in its own interest. It will do anything possible, diplomatically, politically and militarily, to back the revolt, short of provoking either a full-scale war with India or forcing Washington to revive the threat of declaring it a state supporting terrorism (in 1993 Pakistan, on the US State Department's watch-list, narrowly escaped that label). Having talked for so long about freedom and self-determination for the Kashmiris, Pakistani leaders have now begun to articulate their demand for merger, as was done by Prime Minister Benazir Bhutto on her visit to Nepal in May 1994, provoking a critical response from the JKLF. While there have been credible reports in the international media that the average Kashmiri is tired of the violence and disruption of normal life, the long-term prospects of the low-intensity conflict abating are extremely thin.

Governing India: Challenges And Answers
Governing polyglot, multi-ethnic and multi-religious societies has never been easy; different countries and political systems have endeavoured to find their own answers to the challenge. India has

31

followed what may be described as a 'salad bowl approach', according to Nehru's philosophy of unity in diversity. The secular Constitution provides for all distinct ethnicities, linguistic groups and religions. There are 16 official languages and yet there are popular, often violent, agitations by several linguistic groups for official status to be given to their languages.

After its first general elections in 1952, India appointed the States Reorganisation Commission in December 1953, consisting of Saiyad Fazal Ali, H. N. Kunzru and K. M. Panikkar, to look into the demands for statehood based on language, ethnicity, culture and geography. The Commission concluded that it was neither possible nor desirable to recognise states on the basis of a single test of either language or culture, but that a balanced approach to the whole problem was necessary in the interest of national unity. Yet the linguistic formula had become the primary criterion for reorganising states by 1966, partly by design and partly by accident of political act. There have been mixed results, and internal tensions and dissent, but the system has more or less worked. Whenever disaffection has grown into a violent movement, India has responded with a combination of military stick and constitutional carrot, invariably in that order. However, this has had its limitations in Kashmir, and there are stirrings of trouble elsewhere, highlighting the need for caution.

Haphazard economic growth could create new regional imbalances: India's Hindi-speaking political heartland is a good example. Since the region is severed by caste and communal politics, it is likely that much of the fresh investment will be cornered by the more enterprising states such as Maharashtra and Gujarat in the west and Karnataka and Tamil Nadu in the south. This could result in the Hindi heartland, once dominant in national politics, slowly being reduced to supplying cheap labour to the more dynamic states. Already Indian Railways runs special trains from Bihar to Punjab and Haryana as demand for manpower increases in the sowing and harvest seasons.

The importance of economic factors in causing and fuelling alienation cannot be underestimated. A current example is the demand by Jharkhand plains tribals of 21 contiguous districts in the four central and eastern states for statehood for their mineral-rich, but extremely backward region. The movement, launched more than 20 years ago, has only recently acquired electoral strength in the region. In the 1989 general elections, the coalition that ultimately came to power in New Delhi set up a committee to examine the demand in return for electoral arrangements with the Jharkhand Mukti Morcha

(JMM, Jharkhand Liberation Front). Its report, tabled in parliament on 30 March 1992, recommended the formation of a Jharkhand General Council rather than a centrally administered union territory or a state. The government's prevarication led to widespread violence in the region, a rail and road blockade and sabotage. There are some ethnic trappings to the campaign, but the tribals are mainly complaining about the area's backwardness, in view of the fact that it produces a large portion of India's mineral wealth.

Economic concerns are evident in all the likely flashpoints in India, whether it is the demand by Bodo plains tribals in Assam for local autonomy (which has claimed nearly 500 lives in five years), or for statehood by the tribals of Chhatisgarh in Madhya Pradesh, or for Uttaranchal, a separate state for the hill people in Uttar Pradesh. Economics is also central to the extremely bitter Cauvery River waters dispute between Tamil Nadu and Karnataka. In 1993, the row led to the spectacle of the Chief Minister of Tamil Nadu and former film heroine, J. Jayalalitha, joining a 'fast unto death', which was called off only after the Centre intervened. If in the past the challenge was to hold India together in the face of separatist pressures on its periphery, in the future it could take the form of popular movements, violent if not separatist, driven by economic and regional imbalances. Economic reformers will need to monitor the impact of the change at local and regional levels to be able to contain more quickly new imbalances and social irritants.

III. DEFENCE AND SECURITY

Perpetual problems of governance have brought the Indian Army, spotlessly apolitical so far, under increasing pressure. It can be argued that the Indian defence forces have been apolitical to a fault, and submissive to an unhealthy degree in a robust democracy where governance should be a function of the collective thinking of all branches of the state, including the defence forces.[1] In no other major democracy are the armed forces given so insignificant a role in policy-making as in India. In no other democracy do they accept it with the docility evident in India. The Indian defence forces have time and again followed official decisions without even questioning their strategic or tactical soundness.

In 1962 India fought what was essentially a confused politician's war against China, and with disastrous results. The Army accepted the 1984 assault on the Golden Temple as part of *Operation Bluestar* and the 1987 IPKF operations in Sri Lanka without even seeking tactical clarifications. Similarly, the Army has at least twice unquestioningly followed political decisions to cease fire when battles seemed to be turning India's way: the Kashmir campaign in 1948 and the war of attrition in 1965. Service chiefs have frequently been publicly humiliated by politicians or even the bureaucracy. General Sunith Francis Rodrigues, who retired in 1993, was cautioned against speaking to the press in the face of a parliamentary furore after a controversial interview. His predecessor, General V. N. Sharma, swallowed public insult to his troops returning from Sri Lanka when the then Tamil Nadu Chief Minister M. Karunanidhi refused to welcome back 'the murderers of my Tamil brothers'. Over the years, the Army leadership has declined in its overall influence within the power structure, illustrated indirectly by the fact that the last retiring service chief to be appointed state governor or ambassador (a frequent norm in the past) was in 1986.

This might change now, and with wide-ranging consequences, as the Army copes with the debilitating pressures of internal peacekeeping. Bitter lessons were learnt between 1984, when *Operation Bluestar* resulted in a string of mutinies by Sikh soldiers, and 1987, when the troops were made to fight a no-win war without clear political objectives or proper intelligence back-up in Sri Lanka.

Another concern is that the Army is being drawn repeatedly into caste and communal discords, often in recruitment catchment areas, and among the sections of Indian society from which the bulk of its troops is drawn. With such socio-communal tension and polarisation in their villages, the Army would find it difficult to maintain an unassailably impartial and secular image. There is tacit agreement among the forces that it is perfectly justifiable for them to be called out to fight insurgencies or to help during natural disasters, but in most cases, the state governments should be fulfilling their constitutional responsibility of maintaining order rather than rushing for Army help.

Internal discussions on the Army's role in domestic peacekeeping have prompted serious rethinking. The first result was the formation of the National Security Guard, an elite anti-terrorist force under civilian control and patterned on the German GSG-9. Consisting of troops temporarily seconded by the Army and paramilitary, the unit is designed to obviate the need for regular Army forces being called into partisan disputes. This has been followed by the formation and expansion of another paramilitary force, better armed than the existing paramilitary units, called the Rashtriya (National) Rifles.

In fact, despite frequent use of the Army, the size and budgets of central paramilitary forces have burgeoned. The Border Security Force (BJF) was set up in 1965 by drawing up 25 armed police battalions from border states. It now has 140 battalions. The direct correlation with internal troubles is seen by a 55% growth in this paramilitary force in 1981–91, when the Assam, Punjab and Kashmir troubles peaked. The Central Reserve Police Force (CRPF), formed in 1939 as the small Crown Representative Police, a colonial outfit that was rushed to the aid of princely states whenever they were afflicted by civil strife, showed a 35% growth between 1986 and 1991, from 80 battalions to 108 battalions. It is now 119 battalions strong, and growing. The Assam Rifles, established in 1835 as the Cachar Levy to guard British tea gardens in Assam, nearly doubled from 20 to 39 battalions between 1986 and 1991. Between 1986 and 1994, the budgets of all paramilitary forces have more than doubled with the total bill exceeding Rs30bn ($1bn) per year.

However, less and less of these forces are available for the specific tasks for which they were originally created. The bulk of the BSF has now been directed into internal security duties. For nearly 15 years, it has been unable to maintain its prescribed 13-battalion reserve for emergencies. The smaller Indo-Tibetan Border Police (ITBP), specifically raised and trained to police the borders with China along the states of Uttar Pradesh and Himachal Pradesh, has been drawn into policing in the plains. Until 1993, scores of ITBP companies had been deployed to guard banks in Punjab against terrorist depredations. The pressures of internal security have even resulted in the incongruity of battalions of the Nagaland Armed Police being deployed in the heavily wooded foothills of Uttar Pradesh, 2,500 kilometres away, where Sikh militants fleeing from Punjab have been seeking sanctuary – it was only a decade ago that a predominantly Punjabi-led Army was brutally suppressing an insurgency backed by China and Pakistan in Nagaland.

Impatience with internal peacekeeping is evident among senior officers, serving and retired: it takes a crippling toll of the Army's resources and training reserves as well as leaving frontline units fatigued. That is why the Army has resisted the demands of Jammu and Kashmir Governor K. V. Krishna Rao (himself a former Army chief) to deploy two more divisions in the state. In this there are signs of a general increase in the military leadership's role in policy-making. While the Defence Ministry bureaucracy was still dominant, it was significant that a retired general, admiral and air marshal were included in the government's high-level Committee on Defence Expenditures (CDE) in early 1990. Its report has yet to be implemented and the government has been responding evasively to repeated parliamentary directives to do so.[2]

Meanwhile the BJP has keenly pursued Army support and has succeeded in persuading several retired generals (including some prominent war heroes) to join the Party. With 'one rank, one pension' becoming an important election issue, ex-servicemen too have emerged as a bloc vote aggressively wooed by all parties in the Hindi heartland. As a logical consequence, the tenth parliament, elected in June 1991, included many retired soldiers, and their presence has already affected the parliamentary debate on security issues. It is no surprise that parliamentary committees on the Defence Ministry, which have been asking some unusually searching questions in recent years, have had a strong, multi-party representation of former officers. However, the government is still resisting the appointment of serving military officers to the Defence Ministry, and although change is inevitable, it is too early to label this as the beginning of a new Indian military–bureaucratic synthesis.

Force Structures: Learning To Live With Less
Until the late 1980s, India was considered an emerging regional power – more militarily than economically. Between 1985 and 1989 the defence budget rose steeply from 2.9% of GDP to 4.2%, and that, too, in a period of unusually high economic growth. Change since then is mostly attributable to the external policy implications of

domestic developments. Given the preoccupation with internal troubles, the defence forces have had neither the time nor the money to pursue regional power projection. The collapse of the Soviet Union and the end of direct Western involvement in the Afghan conflict in India's neighbourhood have also had an impact.

The 1972 Simla Accord with Pakistan and the improving relationship with China made the 1980s India's second decade since Independence without a full-scale external war (the other being the 1950s). Yet pressures on the armed forces built up at a worrying rate. First, the absence of war was more than compensated for by protracted low-intensity conflict, both internal and in Sri Lanka and the Siachen Glacier, which drained the Indian defence forces. At the same time came a general downswing in the economy in the late 1980s after Rajiv Gandhi's profligate buying of foreign weaponry. The US State Department's Arms Control and Disarmament Agency (ACDA)[3] listed India among the foremost weapon buyers in the world, topping a figure of Rs290bn (nearly US$10bn) for arms imports during the Rajiv Gandhi premiership of 1985–89.

The period also marked the unveiling of an activist foreign policy. India had always shown an inclination for activism, but it was usually confined to diplomacy and the energetic espousal of politically correct causes at multilateral fora. Suddenly the policy was unabashed power projection backed by military muscle. The aggressive military exercises in 1986–87 (*Exercise Brasstacks* and *Exercise Chequerboard* along borders with Pakistan and China, respectively) brought fears of new wars with both old adversaries. This was immediately followed by the disastrous intervention in Sri Lanka after the Rajiv Gandhi–Jayewardene accord to solve the ethnic Tamil problem. And while nearly 60,000 Indian troops were still involved in a bloody guerrilla war in north and north-eastern Sri Lanka, Indian paratroopers also rescued the government of the tiny Indian Ocean archipelago state of Maldives from a coup by an exiled businessman backed by Sri Lankan Tamil mercenaries in 1989.

There was ambitious talk of raising an airborne assault division, rapid mechanisation of the Army with the formation of Reinforced Army Plains and Mountain Divisions (RAPIDS and RAMIDS), acquisition of precision-guided munitions for the Air Force along with the induction of Mirage-2000s and MiG-29s, and even dreams of a blue-water navy. The Navy acquired a new flagship, additional *Harriers* besides Soviet TU-142Ms and, most striking of all, a *Charlie*-class Soviet nuclear-propelled submarine (*Chakra*), which was ultimately returned.

The situation has changed dramatically: all three services are suffering heavily from a shortage of cash and spares, which has affected maintenance and preparedness. War wastage reserves are down to minimum acceptable levels. Mechanisation, creation of RAPIDS and RAMIDS, and expansion of the Navy and the Air Force have all stopped. Crucial long-term acquisition plans, such as the Advanced Jet Trainer (AJT), mobile artillery and a wide range of electronic sensors and countermeasures equipment, have been shelved for want of resources. Once a major buyer in the international arms market, India has not signed one new deal worth $25m or over since 1989. The poor state of maintenance and preparedness is illustrated by the flooding of the engine room of INS *Virat* (formerly HMS *Hermes*), which remained in the dock for nearly six months. In May 1994, the Navy's other aircraft carrier, INS *Vikrant*, had a fire on board, resulting in two deaths. In 1992, the Navy suffered the embarrassment of a Soviet-made corvette sinking in rough seas off the Andaman Islands during a routine exercise.

The other services are not in much better condition. The IAF's Long-Term Re-Equipment Plan (LTREP) has cut down training time to conserve fuel, and all services have greatly curtailed the use of live ammunition during training. The notionally 43-squadron Air Force is effectively down to 37, and it has already begun to 'number-plate' squadrons, whereby aircraft are dispersed to other under-strength squadrons or cannibalised for spares. The Army's plan, drawn up by the ambitious and activist former chief of staff General Krishnaswami Sundarji, had envisaged 80 armoured regiments by 2000. The total in 1994 was 59 and is not expected to increase. Several regiments are short of tanks and certainly lack war reserves. Having been so heavily involved in the domestic troubles, the Army is feeling the impact of them more than the other services.

The three most important reasons for this turnaround are: a growing perception that the medium- and short-term security threats will be internal; budgetary constraints; and the collapse of the Soviet Union, which has supplied most of India's weaponry since the mid-1960s, on easy terms. The trends in India's defence expenditure between 1984 and 1995 indicate the constraints it now faces. After rising consistently and rapidly for five years (from 9.9% of total government expenditure in 1984–85 to 10.3% in 1988–89), the budget was slashed mercilessly in the following four, and despite an increase for 1994–95, the net impact, combined with the 30% devaluation of the rupee in 1992, is considerable. From 4.04% of the GDP in 1986–87, the budget came down to 2.44% in 1993–94 despite sluggish growth in the intervening period, marking a cut of 40%, not accounting for the 1992 devaluation. Since the wage bill has continued to increase, the only areas where expenses can be cut are modernisation and acquisitions. This has led to furious debates on how much India needs to spend for its credible defence in the long run. A widely discussed study by retired Air Commodore Jasjit Singh, who heads the Institute of Defence Studies and Analysis (IDSA),[4] has concluded that India needs to allocate a minimum of 3% of its GDP to ensure credible conventional defence, if geopolitical threats generally remain unchanged in the next decade. A 2.5% GDP spending would be adequate if India were to deploy its nuclear capability, with all the political and international costs that might entail. The study also concludes that even to regain the 1986–87 levels of training and preparedness, the forces will need to spend an additional billion dollars. A recent study conducted by the Army headquarters put the shortfall at Rs120bn (about $4bn) in terms of equipment and ammunition. This was topped by another Rs90bn ($3bn) shortfall for housing.

While suspension of acquisitions and modernisation is a problem, the services have begun to complain about the dangers of slashing expenditure on exercises and training. It is here that the burdens of low-intensity conflict and internal peacekeeping become most taxing. The Army, for example, has been asking if a way could be found to pay for its internal duties other than from its share of the budget. It has already spent nearly Rs15m ($0.5m) per day on operations in the Siachen Glacier in Kashmir. The Air Force transport fleet is running up unaffordable costs and wear and tear, besides engine hours on its transport fleet ferrying military and paramilitary forces between troubled regions. One suggestion under consideration is to make the states pay directly for the cost of peacekeeping by central paramilitary forces and the Army. This will have the additional benefit of discouraging requisition of the Army at the slightest provocation.

It was only in early 1993 that the military leadership began to accept budgetary constraints in their long-term planning. Several exercises are now under way to cut expenses and raise resources. The Defence Ministry told the Parliament's Standing Committee on Defence for 1994–95, that it had already effected a saving of Rs1,980m ($66m) by 'rationalisation' of non-combatant manpower in the Army.[5] Another Rs3,000m ($100m) is claimed to have been saved by the use of simulators for training, and the modernisation of inventory management and introduction of a central inventory control system is said to have saved another Rs960m (about $32m). The Ministry claimed that, overall, these measures saved Rs11,494.9m ($380m) in 1992, Rs7,607.2m ($253m) the following year and the estimate for 1994–95 is Rs7,500m ($250m). The Defence Ministry is considering a proposal by the Army to sell some of its enormous holdings of lands in colonial-period cantonments spread all over the country. The money thus raised could be used to build housing for troops. Efforts were made to cut down expense on support services by assigning forward-dumping of fuel and lubricants to the state-owned Indian Oil Corporation on a commercial basis and even to give out major vehicle maintenance and repair contracts to existing private companies. All three forces have embarked on a process of mothballing surplus equipment and are seeking Israeli expertise to do so.

After avoiding the issue for many years, India's defence planners are conducting a serious review of recruitment policies to keep future salary and pension bills within manageable limits. According to some estimates, the pension bill may outstrip the defence budget within a decade. Indian defence forces are voluntary and most personnel serve long periods and are thus entitled to pensions. One proposal is a seven-year service, whereby soldiers would normally retire after seven years and would then be absorbed in paramilitary and state police forces. This would reduce the pension burden, help to keep the Army young, and also provide paramilitary forces with better-quality manpower. Yet the defence establishment is hesitant to make a commitment on substantial manpower cuts despite an unequivocal recommendation by the Estimates Committee of Parliament for 1992–93 and 1993–94.[6] The Committee upbraided the Ministry for its 'casual' and 'evasive' attitude and argued that 'considering the present trend throughout the world, of making the armed forces technology intensive, the Committee finds little rationale behind the manpower ceiling remaining stationary during the last decade'. But three successive Army chiefs have stated publicly that there is no way they could sustain the present force structures and recruitment patterns in the next decade, and it is only a matter of time before manpower cuts begin in earnest. It is significant that in spite of the large size of its armed forces (nearly 1.5m, including the paramilitary units), a recent study of 34 Asian nations by the IDSA, ranked India thirty-third in terms of soldiers per thousand of the population. As the armed forces' contribution to the creation of employment in such a large population is rather small, manpower reductions will not provoke a serious outcry. In fact, successive parliamentary committees have expressed frustration at the defence forces' hesitation over making these cuts.

Impact On Defence Industry And Procurement
The impact of budgetary cuts and the unfavourable exchange rate has been compounded by the Soviet collapse. For the defence establishment, the loss of Moscow as an ally means the loss of the old terms of armament purchases: nominal prices, barter and rupee payment with easy credits. This causes further problems with supplies of spares, ammunition and fulfilling maintenance contracts. Practically all the Army's frontline armour and mechanised units use Soviet-made equipment. This also forms an important part of the artillery and constitutes the entire anti-aircraft artillery including the panoply of surface-to-air missile (SAM) batteries. All but seven of the 43 IAF squadrons use versions of MiGs, *Ilyushins* and the Mi-series helicopters, and most of the Navy's submarine and destroyer/missile boat division is built around Soviet equipment.

Given the large build-up of stocks and the traditional reliance on Soviet equipment, it is difficult for India suddenly to find other sources of weapons procurement. And if this is unavoidable, where is the cash to pay for wholesale replacement of equipment, especially at Western prices? India, characteristically, is looking for a middle path. High-level delegations have been sent to Russia and other former Soviet republics, particularly Ukraine, to ensure supplies of ammunition and spares. Indeed, a promise was made by Russian President Boris Yeltsin on his visit to India in 1992 and repeated during Rao's visit to Moscow in July 1994. However, even the conservative Indian establishment has finally accepted the need to resort to unconventional measures, such as sending delegations to buy spares for cash in dollars. The services of private export–import houses have been requisitioned to maintain Russian/Eastern bloc arms supplies as businessmen, operating in the region for decades, have better contacts at the dealer level and an understanding of Soviet business practices. India has no option but to try to maintain the tenuous Russian supply-line, and this was one of the main items on Rao's Moscow agenda.

It was a measure of the confusion prevailing that while Indian forces were desperate for supplies, several independent companies attempted to sell equipment to India. Notable among these was a proposal by the Indian government for Hindustan Aeronautics Ltd, a state-owned company, to undertake the $100m retrofit of nearly a hundred MiG-21bis in frontline IAF squadrons to upgrade their

41

avionics, range and radar. Indicating its hope of continuing the highly useful relationship with Moscow, India has preferred the Russian offer despite competitive bids from elsewhere, particularly Israel. India also agreed in principle to buy another 30 MiG-29s, including six two-seat trainers. The Navy, too, is seriously looking at the 44,000-tonne Ukrainian aircraft carrier as a replacement for INS *Vikrant*, which is overdue for retirement.

The sizeable domestic armament industry has been crippled. The heavy vehicles factory at Avadi near Madras, with the capability to make 400 T-72 tanks a year, now has orders for barely 75. Similarly, the factory at Medak, in Andhra Pradesh, built to produce 350 BMP-2 infantry combat vehicles annually, has orders for merely 100. The Army needs more pieces, but has no money to buy them. Even where orders have been placed, the indigenous industry is bedevilled by foreign-exchange shortages. The public-sector corporation Bharat Electronics is unable to deliver more than one-quarter of the 100 low-level radars ordered by the forces each year because of the paucity of foreign exchange to import essential components.[7] Hindustan Aeronautics Ltd, also in the public sector, is the worst hit. With the drying up of the Jaguar, MiG-21, -23, -27 and Dornier-228 orderbooks, its chairman R. N. Sharma has been bidding for international maintenance contracts even if it means 'becoming a service department rather than a production unit'.[8]

India's predicament would not have been so serious if its defence research and development plans had come to fruition. The Army had expected the Indian-designed and built main battle tank (MBT) *Arjun* to enter service by 1988 at the latest. It still has design, weight and mobility problems and now seems unlikely to enter service before 1996. Similarly, the light combat aircraft (LCA) programme has suffered from time and cost over-runs. And while the government fully supports the programme (budgetary support continues at planned levels), it is widely accepted in the defence establishment that the project could be cancelled. The Navy's renewed interest in the Ukrainian carrier also indicates an impatience with the Defence Research and Development Organisation's (DRDO) aircraft-carrier project, and proves that a used Soviet-origin vessel is more affordable than a new, indigenously produced carrier. Ironically, the one programme that has matured and is ready for induction has had to be held in abeyance because of financial constraints. The Indian Army had decided almost a decade ago to shift from 7.62mm to 5.56mm small arms in keeping with the international trend towards greater mobility and higher volumes of fire. The Armament Research and

Development Establishment (ARDE), based in the western industrial city of Pune, has successfully completed what is called the Indian Small Arms Systems (INSAS) programme, but there simply is not enough money to set up production facilities. As a stop-gap measure, some special forces, particularly those employed in counter-insurgency and close-quarter battle situations, have been re-equipped with hurriedly imported AK series weapons from Eastern Europe. Some are also being re-equipped with large stores of AK series weaponry captured from Kashmir and Punjab militants.

The Missile And Nuclear Programmes

Budgetary cuts have not affected the Integrated Guided Missile Development Programme (IMGDP). In fact, in the 1994–95 budget, the government raised its allocation for defence research and development by Rs210m (about $7m) and its outlay on ordnance factories by Rs42m ($1.4m). The programme has already cost Rs8,000m ($266m). Five different guided missiles are being developed: *Agni* (fire), an intermediate-range ballistic missile (IRBM); *Prithvi* (the earth), a tactical short- to medium-range surface-to-surface missile (SSM); *Akash* (the sky), a *Patriot*-class SAM with phased-array radar; *Trishul* (trident), a short-range fully autonomous system akin to the Soviet SA-8; and *Nag* (cobra), an anti-tank missile capable of being used from multiple platforms. The programme was headed by Dr A. P. J. Kalam, now head of the Defence Research and Development Organisation and scientific adviser to the Defence Minister.[9] All five systems are in various stages of trial, and only *Prithvi* can be considered anywhere near deployment. *Agni*, which has attracted the most international attention because of its IRBM capabilities, is still at prototype stage and the other three are far from production.

The importance attached to India's missile programme explains the continuous financial investment and a steadfast refusal to bow to American pressure to suspend or even slow it down. It has now acquired the same kind of multi-partisan political support as the nuclear programme. Rao did make a political gesture to the US by putting off a *Prithvi* test a week before his visit to Washington in May 1994, but this resulted in a furore in parliament and the media and, amid allegations of a sell-out, the government had to hold not one, but two tests a month later. Dr Kalam was even quoted in early 1994 as saying that India had progressed so far in its missile development that the government could now go ahead and sign the Missile Technology Control Regime (MTCR).[10]

However, the programme still suffers from paucity of crucial component supplies, technology and doctrinal problems and, indeed, financial constraints. It would be rash to accept the official claims, ignoring the consistent failure of the Indian defence research establishment to put into production any significant weapons system that it develops. Because of a combination of these factors, including the MTCR, it is unlikely that any missile other than *Prithvi* will be deployed in any considerable strength by 1997. Even the *Prithvi* deployment will be small and symbolic (the Army's first order is for only 75) and *Agni* is unlikely to proceed beyond the prototype stage. A missile of *Agni*'s range and capabilities can only be worthwhile if it carries a nuclear warhead, and unless India nuclearises its weapon systems – a remote possibility – it will not see any sense in deploying this missile, given the expense and international pressures it will generate. This will, however, remain a point of contention in India–US relations.

A similar situation will persist in the nuclear programme. After a complicated series of sometimes impatient exchanges between 1992 and 1994 period, when US non-proliferation fundamentalism gathered support, India now feels that it has persuaded Washington to appreciate the reasons behind its opposition to signing the Nuclear Non-Proliferation Treaty (NPT). US officials have said quite openly – and the State Department mentioned it in its 1993–94 report to Congress on nuclear proliferation – that it would be political suicide for any government in New Delhi to sign the NPT. The US effort now is to persuade both India and Pakistan to cap their nuclear and missile capabilities. India reacted violently to suggestions in Washington for a one-time waiver on the Pressler Amendment (blocking the sale of armaments to Pakistan if it persisted with a nuclear-weapons programme), to supply Pakistan with 38 F-16s in return for a verifiable guarantee on nuclear capping. India's outrage brought US Deputy Secretary of State Strobe Talbott to New Delhi in April 1994, and Rao's Washington visit followed in mid-May.

In 1993, India and the US held several meetings on the issue besides exchanging official notes and 'non-papers'. The US, knowing India's aversion to foreign intervention in what it sees as bilateral issues within the subcontinent, tried to widen the nuclear debate by proposing a meeting of the five nuclear powers, as well as India, Pakistan, Germany and Japan. India opposed this as well, refusing to be drawn into any discussion in which China (seen as a long-term nuclear threat) was not participating as an equal. In March 1994, on a visit to the UK, Rao expanded the debate by seeking participation with similar status for other 'regional nuclear powers', such as Russia. Indian officials later added Kazakhstan to the list.

While stalling US requests for a multinational debate, India has been pushing its own formulation, topped by the suggestion of a no-first-use agreement with Pakistan, to be followed by confidence-building measures, again purely at a bilateral level. Rao articulated this in his May address to the joint session of the US Congress, underlining every nation's 'sovereign right' to decide its own defence requirements, the need for global disarmament and, for the moment, wherever fears of nuclear conflagration exist, a no-first-use agreement to 'prevent accidental conflagration'.

It would, however, be hasty to conclude that the Indian nuclear policy in the 1990s will see no shift from the past. Fundamentally, it may remain similar to the old two-track policy of keeping the nuclear option open while negotiating for a universal, non-discriminatory non-proliferation regime, along the lines of the chemical weapons convention rather than the NPT. But changes may take place in various aspects of this broad policy in the coming years, firstly due to increased pressures from the US, coinciding with the 1995 NPT renewal, and then through the possible use of allurements, such as permanent membership of the United Nations (UN) in return for nuclear concessions. It is significant that all the candidates for permanent membership if the Security Council is restructured (Germany, Brazil, Japan and India) have a recessed nuclear capability.[11] At the same time, India's rather stubborn position, accepting neither the NPT nor a regional non-proliferation regime, such as in Latin America, will be tested. Some indication of how India might deal with this is given by the key trends in its largely reactive nuclear policy. The impetus for an Indian 'device' clearly came from the defeat by China in 1962, followed by the Chinese nuclear test in 1964. The view that India needed at least recessed deterrence was cemented during the Bangladesh War in 1971 when the US sent its Seventh Fleet Task Force to the Bay of Bengal to compel India to an early cease-fire.

The strategy of flaunting a nuclear capability but stopping short of nuclearisation indicates that while India is willing to exercise the extreme option in case its security is gravely jeopardised, it is not willing to pay the price for full nuclearisation in terms of international opprobrium and sanctions. The missile programme is an extension of the same policy: it displays India's delivery capability, adding a logical dimension to nuclear status, and yet it will resist deploying the most powerful of these missiles.

India will continue to assert that it needs nuclear deterrence, primarily against China, but its strategists will be worried about Pakistan, with which India has a chronic worry in Kashmir. Given the conventional force structures in the region and the improbability of total air superiority, it is difficult to envisage India trying to destroy Pakistan's nuclear capability by conventional means in the foreseeable future. But the missile programme is also a message to Pakistan that India could still manage to stay ahead in the race. At another level, should a real phase of arms-control negotiations begin, missiles will become a vital bargaining tool.

In the subcontinent, the end of the Cold War has given impetus to nuclear ambitions. India fears being a peripheral power in a unipolar world. Pakistan fears being left without superpower protection in a future conflict with India. India's motives in challenging the traditional definition of the 'region' and expanding the nuclear debate to include Central Asia and Russia, and indeed China, are obvious. It wants to bide its time, internationalise the proliferation debate on the eve of the NPT renewal and, in the unlikely event of having to make nuclear trade-offs under international pressure, to extract as much denuclearisation from as wide a region around its borders as possible.

At the domestic level, if the Army were to be more involved in shaping the strategy, the nuclear stance would harden. The Army has consistently demanded nuclear weapons since the mid-1960s but so far it has more or less been excluded from the nuclear programme.[12] However, the pressure from top military officials at least to let the Army help to develop tactics is bound to increase. And while India's conventional forces have some capability to fight in nuclear, biological and chemical (NBC) conditions, with the nuclear threat becoming clearer, the defence forces will expect an improvement on this.

At the doctrinal level, there appears to be a subtle shift in the traditional Indian position. The articulation of a 'no-first-use' policy, at least in the Pakistani case, seems to indicate that India may be building the potential for a second-strike capability. The most conservative estimate of weapon-grade fissile material is that India now has the capability to manufacture at least 60 bombs. This is about the number needed to create a second-strike capability against Pakistan.[13]

However, a serious public debate on the targeting strategy has yet to take place. Despite three bitter wars, both India and Pakistan have desisted from targeting civilian centres, and the fighting has mainly been limited to the combatants. This illustrates a difference between the military strategy on the subcontinent and, for instance, Western Europe, where civilian centres have been considered legitimate military targets at least since the Second World War. Hence the dilemma for Indian and Pakistani military planners is whether the accepted Western nuclear counter-city doctrine is to be adopted, or whether the two sides will evolve only a counter-force strategy. The signs so far are that neither side has considered such a doctrine: the Indian Army is expected to use the nuclear-capable *Prithvi* only against military targets, such as airfields and troop concentrations. The only indication of this policy is the agreement between the two countries not to attack each other's nuclear capabilities, which, interestingly, are located right next to or in the middle of centres with large populations.

Options For The Future
Serious rethinking in the defence establishment began with the setting up of the high-level Committee on Defence Expenditures (CDE), headed by former Minister of State for Defence Research and Development, Arun Singh. The Committee looked at the entire gamut of planning: security doctrines; the composition of the forces; leadership and command structures; civilian–military interface; budgeting and spending powers; and large-scale cost cuts and optimisation of resources. It recommended integration of Army, Navy and Air Force headquarters and the creation of a Vice-Chief of Defence Staff (VCDS) to be drawn from any of the three branches and to represent the forces in the Defence Ministry with direct access to the Defence Minister. The Committee recommended automatic annual increases in the defence budget to offset inflation, enhanced financial powers to service chiefs to channel funds directly, and considerable cost cuts by reducing static or administrative units left over from the raj. The civilian bureaucracy, which thus stands to lose its overriding powers, has successfully stalled implementation of these recommendations for more than two years.

To counter shrinking budgets, even arms export is being considered. In the past, India was extremely shy of entering the arms market as a seller, even though it was such a major buyer. Its arms exports have rarely crossed the $5m per year mark, which is surprisingly little for so large a military-industrial establishment. This was caused by two factors: compulsions imposed by non-aligned politics and India's aggressive espousal of idealistic international causes from multinational fora; and the simple fact that the defence industry is within the inefficient state-owned sector, which can hardly be accused of being driven by a profit motive. India's idiosyncratic international politics constrained even such straightforward decisions as selling old equipment. In the mid-1970s, more than 100 obsolete Centurion tanks were sold to a scrap dealer in South Africa; New Dehli was embarrassed when reports surfaced that the racist regime had reconditioned the tanks and was using them against the Blacks whose cause India so strongly espoused. In the late 1980s India refused to sell two squadrons of Jaguars to Thailand, even though the state-owned Hindustan Aeronautics Ltd (HAL) was being forced to shut the licensed-production line for the strike aircraft after IAF orders had been executed. The argument was that Thailand had an adversarial relationship with Vietnam.

Against this background, and given the current state of international arms business, it is unlikely that India could effect a major breakthrough. Some planners, however, are now looking at export of services. In late 1992, the then Defence Minister, Sharad Pawar, visited Kuala Lumpur and signed a ground-breaking agreement for servicing and maintaining Malaysian MiG-29s and training the crews. India has also offered to train Kuwaiti defence forces at its training establishments.[14]

The chairman of HAL has been talking in terms of setting up multinational joint ventures, and since 1993 the company has taken the lead in helping to organise an annual international aviation trade fair (Avia India) in Bangalore. It is now discussing joint venture proposals with Israel (for the pilotless target aircraft), and even China, for civilian transport aircraft.[15] The company has also offered its facilities for maintaining the aircraft, mainly Boeing 737s, flown by the 11 small private airlines that have been formed since the government's 1992 open-skies policy and loosening of the public-sector monopoly over civil aviation.

Overall, India must rethink its fundamental security doctrine and planning. It was partly because of the recent constraints that the Army was so enthusiastic about the Rao government's historic agreement with China to freeze the border issue and to initiate a process of mutual disengagement of forces and withdrawals. Such change will be calibrated, but ultimately the result will be smaller, leaner forces. The crucial debate in India is whether its strategists presume that there is no possibility of war for a decade or so, and then set about enforcing long-term restructuring and reorganisation. The problem is that continuing trouble in Kashmir and tension on the borders with Pakistan have created a situation in which Indian planners have constantly to provide for near-warlike readiness; consequently there is no breathing space to begin long-term rethinking. Given the realities on the ground in Kashmir, this situation is likely to persist.

While qualitative and quantitative changes in doctrine, force structures and recruitment policies are inevitable, they will necessarily be slow and stretch over a long period. A crucial question is how this will influence both India's old desire for power projection, at least within its immediate geopolitical environment, and belief in the prestige of military muscle, even if not employed aggressively to back diplomatic moves. The slow pace of change will probably force Indian policy-makers to consider a different route, which has already been evident in the way Rao conducted his diplomacy in 1993–94 in the US, the UK, France, Germany and Singapore.

IV. REGIONAL CHANGE AND EXTERNAL POLICIES

The most notable shift in India's perception of threat is the manner in which it has become inward-looking. In the past, India was compelled to maintain a two-front army, facing China and Pakistan, with additional concern over the superpower naval presence in the Indian Ocean. The changing equation with China is diminishing worries along the Tibetan borders. Similarly, increasing US diplomatic activism and Pakistan's susceptibility to pressure from Washington has also reduced the possibility of a conventional war with that old adversary. Yet, while the external situation has largely improved, internal insecurities continue to run high; and when internal troubles are augmented by external threats they become most serious. Kashmir is a good example: Pakistan, today, would not be seen as a danger if a rebellion had not been raging there.

This picture becomes further clouded by Islamic fundamentalism. So far the Indian Muslims outside Kashmir have not made common cause with the Valley Muslims. But following Ayodhya and the subsequent rioting, there is widespread insecurity and alienation among the large Muslim population in India. In several cities, most notably Bombay, Muslims have been drawn into terrorism to take 'revenge' for the riots. This combines with internal troubles in Kashmir and Pakistan to create the most serious security threat to India. Given secularist compulsions, New Delhi can neither tackle this directly nor ignore it. If it cracks down on Muslim fundamentalists, it further angers an alienated minority and gives the BJP a propaganda victory; if it ignores the situation, militancy might continue to rise. The predicament is illustrated by India's failure to counter Pakistan's allegations of an ethnic cleansing of the Valley Muslims. All it need do is to point to the actual ethnic cleansing in the Valley of the 385,000-strong Hindu Pandit community that has been driven out to refugee camps in Jammu and New Delhi. But by highlighting this, it would be conceding political ground to the BJP by lending credence to its claim that Hindus are being persecuted.

Changing Regional Equations

The Indian subcontinent has been no more than a distant spectator of the two most significant international events of the recent past: the 1991 Gulf War and the break-up of the Soviet Union and Eastern Europe. None of the countries in the region, including India and Pakistan (which are the only real power players), had any military, political or ideological role in the developments – Pakistan's small involvement in the allied force in the Gulf was at most symbolic. And yet these changes have completely rewritten the security equation in the subcontinent, regionalising threat perceptions and stripping the long-standing subcontinental conflicts of their Cold War trappings. As the nations discover friends and enemies in a strange new world, the change has generated a comprehensive rethinking that could lead to a new set of policies and balance of power.

This is not to say that in the past the conflict in the region was a direct extension of the Cold War, but it was substantially exacerbated by it. By the mid-1950s, the US had chosen Pakistan as a key player in the anti-communist alliance in regions close to China and the Soviet Union. The Indian leadership, dominated by Nehruvian thought, was in any case more inclined towards socialism, and as relations between Moscow and Beijing soured and India's own problems with China increased, the subcontinent became a vital concern of the Cold Warriors. By the mid-1960s, the divide was complete, with the US and the West backing Pakistan on Kashmir and India relying on the Soviet veto to block UN plebiscite resolutions on Kashmir. The 1971 war marked a watershed, with India signing the 20-year treaty of peace, friendship and cooperation with Moscow, which included a provision for immediate consultations in case either country was under external threat. Meanwhile, Pakistan drew even closer to the US in the 1971 Kissinger–Nixon overture to Beijing. Now the scene has changed dramatically.

More recently, the nearest the two nations came to a conflict was in spring 1990, when tensions over Kashmir reached a high pitch and the US administration suspected, on the evidence of spy satellites, that Pakistan was preparing for a nuclear conflict by arming its F-16s with its nuclear weapons.[1] How the subcontinent was brought back from this dangerous brinkmanship is explained by the way strategic equations have evolved. Unlike in the past, increasing tensions did not elicit the 'expected' reactions from the superpowers: both the Soviet Union and the US, rather than rally to the side of their respective allies in the subcontinent, unanimously counselled restraint. The US immediately employed its considerably greater diplomatic leverage in Islamabad to lessen the rhetoric, and visiting Moscow in January an Indian delegation, led by the then Foreign Secretary S. K. Singh, was firmly told that while the Soviets would continue to supply weapon systems and spares still in the pipeline, India could no longer count on unquestioning political support in case of a conflict.[2] The US intervened at an unprecedentedly high level by sending a powerful delegation led by the then Deputy National Security adviser and later CIA Chief Robert Gates. With the superpowers unwilling to take sides in subcontinental conflicts, India and Pakistan were left on their own without external advice, inspiration or arbitration. This happened a year before the 1991 Gulf War, which brought about even greater change along the same coordinates.

Within the region, recent years have seen tremendous strides by democratic movements. In Pakistan, despite the continuing notion of invisible hands – mostly the Army's – indirectly controlling levers of power and policy, there is no denying that electoral democracy has emerged stronger from the 1993 elections, which were widely hailed as the cleanest ever. In India, the democratic system held firm, despite the assassination of Rajiv Gandhi, and by the end of 1993 New Delhi had its first government with a clear majority of its own in parliament in four years.

Bangladesh has seen the end of dictatorship and so far a reasonably stable elected government under Khaleda Zia, widow of the assassinated former dictator. Sri Lanka has also been able to restore peace at least in its southern Sinhala political mainland while recovering from a string of assassinations, including that of its president, Ranasinghe Premadasa, in 1993. Even the tiny Himalayan kingdom of Bhutan has seen the stirrings of democracy. All the major countries of the region have also embarked on programmes of economic reform.

Generally, these circumstances should make for greater harmony within the region and greater interface with India, which, after the activist diplomacy of the 1980s, is now a sober, more inward-looking regional power. But problems remain at the populist level as a neighbour as large and powerful as India inevitably casts a vast shadow on electoral politics in much smaller countries. In Nepal and Bangladesh, for example, harnessing and sharing river waters with India has become a crucial and sensitive election issue, and the two governments have been forced to adopt a confrontational posture to satisfy their voting constituencies.

While these irritants persist the region is held to ransom by the India–Pakistan relationship. Over the past decade or so this has been a troubled union, with fleeting interludes of affection in an endless series of rows stopping just short of divorce. Three times in the past decade (1984, 1987 and 1990) the two neighbours came close to war. And at least twice, reconciliation looked possible: during the Rajiv Gandhi–Benazir Bhutto 'honeymoon' for about a year beginning with the SAARC summit in Islamabad in December 1988; and then in the early days of Mian Nawaz Sharif's premiership. An agreement not to attack each other's nuclear facilities was signed and ratified, and talks on disengaging forces from the Siachen Glacier broke down just when the agreement seemed to have been reached.

Overall, the relationship has been sliding since the mid-1980s. India believes that Pakistani interference is the primary cause behind its internal problems, and that it is now embarking on another phase of subversion by exploiting the Indian Muslim's post-Ayodhya insecurities to create gangs of saboteurs in India's urban and industrial centres. The specific targeting of economic centres, including the Stock Exchange and the Air India headquarters, is seen as an example of this. The Indian view is that Pakistan's acquisition of a nuclear deterrent to deny India the option of conventional war has emboldened it to continue with the low-intensity conflict and, the term Indian spokesmen use so often, 'proxy war'. Pakistan, on the other hand, has revanchist pressures of its own, given the history of the Indian involvement in the Bangladesh rebellion.

A claim on the entire Kashmir region is also the central feature of its national policy, and this policy finds total unanimity across the political spectrum. It is therefore unlikely that a Pakistani government, even if it wanted to, would be able to take a conciliatory approach to the issue. The rhetoric on the Pakistani side has become increasingly shrill with demands for UN intervention and repudiation of the 1972 Simla Accord. This agreement resulted in the return of nearly 96,000 prisoners taken during the Bangladesh War to Pakistan and had clauses on peaceful and bilateral resolution of all issues, including Kashmir. The Indian understanding of the agreement, which redefined the cease-fire line in Kashmir as the Line of Control (LoC), is that it freezes the Kashmir issue, giving the LoC the status of a *de facto* border; and that any effort to discuss Kashmir outside the bilateral India–Pakistan framework is a violation of the accord. Pakistan believes that India has not kept its promise by procrastinating on discussing Kashmir, and hence it has no choice but to go to the international community. By early 1994 Pakistan had begun publicly to dissociate from the accord, and its Foreign Minister, Sardar Assef Ali, was quoted in the media as saying that the 'Simla Accord is a dead document'.[3]

India, partly as a conscious policy and partly in reaction to US pressures, has been keener than Pakistan to maintain a dialogue. In a remarkable shift from its earlier stand, it agreed to discuss the Kashmir issue 'in its entirety' and to persuade Pakistan into yet another round of talks between foreign secretaries. Nothing substantive was achieved in those held in December 1993. In fact, relations hit a new low as Pakistan persisted with its threat to move a resolution censuring India's human-rights record in Kashmir at the Human Rights Convention in Geneva in March 1994. It is a sign of the changing times that India was ultimately able to persuade China and Iran, two of Pakistan's closest friends in the region, to put pressure on Pakistan to withdraw the resolution just before it came up for voting. At one level, the incident was seen as a victory of Indian diplomacy. At another, it was a victory for Pakistan, which had managed to internationalise the issue to the extent that it was discussed at the Convention, and India, as a damage-control measure, was forced to allow easy access to Kashmir to foreign diplomats and international humanitarian organisations, such as the International Commission of the Red Cross (ICRC) and International Commission of Jurists (ICJ).

The most significant move in the relationship was made by India in the first week of February 1994 with the submission of six 'non-papers' to Pakistan, suggesting a new regime of confidence-building measures. These included a commitment by each country not to employ its nuclear capability against the other; disengagement of forces on the Siachen Glacier to a predesignated line without prejudice to either side's territorial claims; establishment of better and more secure communication between the armed forces to exchange information about troop movements and exercises; and even a proposal to solve the tiny territorial waters dispute over Sir Creek in the Arabian Sea. Pakistan responded to the proposal after a long delay, arguing that there was no point talking about non-use of nuclear capability as it had none, and that unless the central question of Kashmir was tackled first, there was nothing to be gained by discussing other issues which it saw as peripheral.

There is no prospect of the diplomatic skirmishing and the low-intensity conflict in Kashmir easing in the near future, just as there is no prospect of an all-out war unless Pakistan increases hostilities so much in Kashmir that India has no option but to retaliate in an open, conventional war in the plains. The situation will continue to cause concern and impatience in Western capitals, particularly Washington. Given the history of India–Pakistan relations, however, there are strict limits to what outside intervention can achieve in terms of lasting peace. On the three occasions when such an effort was made, they proved to be a failure. The UN-sponsored cease-fire in Kashmir in 1948 was observed mostly in its breach. The British-backed peace accord following the dispute over the Kutch marshlands on the Indo-Pakistan border in April 1965 was followed by a full-scale war three months later; in the 1971 war, India recaptured the Kutch territories given to Pakistan in the accord, officially repudiating it. And the Soviet-sponsored Tashkent summit and accord in January 1966 could not prevent an even bigger war five years later. The longest period of peace – 22 years to date – has been made possible by a purely bilateral summit and accord at Simla between Indira Gandhi and Zulfiqar Ali Bhutto.

The instrument for long-term peace in the future, too, has to be bilateralism, all the more so as there will always remain a deep suspicion in the subcontinent of any accord brokered by outsiders. Against this background, outside powers can only help by firmly and constantly counselling restraint and nudging both countries towards a dialogue. In the 1992–93 period, for example, the US threat to put Pakistan on the list of states supporting terrorism had a salutary effect – it stopped aid to Sikh militants and slowed down Pakistani activism in Kashmir. Such activity has picked up again with the Pakistani intelligence agency, Inter Services Intelligence (ISI), embarking on a long-term plan to privatise aid to Kashmiri militants through pan-Islamic organisations left over from the Afghan war with Pakistani Jamaat-i-Islami in the vanguard. Official Pakistani spokesmen have admitted that it is 'impossible' to stop altogether such assistance.[4] Even the US view, stated by President Clinton at his joint White House news conference with Rao in May 1994, is that 'some aid' is now being 'provided by private organisations'. Kashmir determining the status of the India–Pakistan relationship, which in turn dictates the level of South Asian regional cooperation, is a cycle unlikely to be broken in the foreseeable future.

Elsewhere in the region, India has tried to depart from the activist foreign policy of Mrs Gandhi. In May 1992, Rao and Bangladesh Prime Minister Khaleda Zia signed an agreement over the vexed river-waters issue and also gave Dhaka access to some of its land-locked enclave territories. The river-waters problem again defied solution, but the relationship, overall, has improved with the most recent Indian budget offering duty concessions on Bangladeshi goods. Indo-Sri Lankan relations continued to improve and there were no new tensions; trade grew by 23% in 1992 and 24% the following year. This must be seen in the context of a populist boycott of Indian goods in Sri Lanka in the recent past. India offered duty-free status to Nepalese goods, provided that at least 50% of labour used was Nepalese, but the key question of joint exploitation of river-water resources still remains unanswered. India raised rates on electricity purchased from Bhutan by 40% – a significant sop considering that power exports constitute 40% of the hill kingdom's GDP. Even with Pakistan, ironically, trade continued to increase, extending to 571 items (compared to 52 in 1985) and Pakistan retained a favourable trade-balance – $77m in 1992. At the same time, SAARC was bedevilled by contentious bilateral problems within its member-states. Yet India needs to show greater magnanimity in its dealings with its neighbours. Irritants such as frequent transgressions of Nepalese territory by Indian police teams must be avoided. Because of its size, India will be viewed with suspicion by its much smaller neighbours, and India's policy-makers must be sensitive to these insecurities.

The China Factor

Within the region, the most important development is the Sino-Indian thaw, evident in the wide-ranging agreement between the Asian giants to freeze the border issue, embark on a programme of mutual disengagement and troop withdrawals, institute confidence-building measures and increase trade and cultural relations. The agreement was signed during Rao's visit to China in autumn 1993, but the process began with Rajiv Gandhi's visit to China in 1988, and Chinese Premier Li Peng's visit to India in December 1991. The accord was followed up promptly by talks between top officials and generals from both sides and the contact picked up again in 1994. Withdrawals have not yet been formally initiated, but India has begun moving out heavier artillery and combat air squadrons, signalling an easing of the situation. The only discordant note in the process was sounded by Chinese Vice-Premier and Foreign Affairs Minister Qian Qichen on his visit to India in July 1994, when he suggested that withdrawals should be initiated by the party that moved the forces first into the area. This echoed old Chinese allegations that India was the aggressor in 1962 and ran contrary to the recent conciliatory spirit.

Meanwhile, the business relationship improves. In 1987, Sino-Indian trade amounted to just Rs3,522m ($117.4m). In 1993–94, it had crossed the Rs2,100m ($700m) mark and was placed marginally higher than the figure for Pakistan–China trade. This is expected to double in the next three years. The growing warmth has led to suggestions in certain circles, mainly among old leftists and socialists in India, that the two Asian neighbours could form a strong alliance against US domination of world politics and trade. But this is implausible, partly because there is little convergence of international interest between India and China, partly because China is unlikely to see India as an equal partner in such an alliance, and also because neither country wishes to be considered anti-Western or anti-US. When ideological obstacles have disappeared and economic interests beckon them towards the West, neither Beijing nor New Delhi will want to take a confrontational position.

Yet the thaw has already brought India regional dividends. Beijing's new stance on Kashmir, supporting a bilateral solution based on the Simla Accord and its neutrality on Pakistan's Kashmir campaign at international fora, is a gain for India. The relationship is likely to proceed with a much higher economic content. In the medium term, the only contentious issue between the neighbours is the activities of the exiled Dalai Lama and his followers, and New Delhi has gone out of its way to control these. When an independent forum of parliamentarians organised a Free Tibet conference in New Delhi in February 1994, not only did the government not participate, it firmly discouraged ruling party leaders from even the slightest involvement.

The almost total lack of opposition in parliament, in the media and even from former generals to what is seen as acceptance of the *de facto* border with China (according to Indian claims, China occupies nearly 12,000 square miles of their territory), is as surprising as it is significant. It shows, primarily, that in the Indian psyche so dominant is the threat from Pakistan, combined with internal troubles, that the continuation of tension with China is an unnecessary distraction. The Chinese, too, have tried to address India's internal security concerns by making reassuring noises. In April 1994, the Chinese Ambassador to India stated at a news conference in Calcutta that his country was considering formally accepting Sikkim's accession to India – something Beijing had bitterly contested until then. He also said that there was no question of China backing any insurgencies in India in future and that it wanted India and Pakistan to solve the Kashmir problem bilaterally. The Ministry of External Affairs has its legion of Sino-sceptics, but currently Indian policy-makers are encouraged by such assurances. The turnaround in relations is remarkable considering that as recently as 1987 the Asian giants were responding belligerently to India's charge that China had occupied tiny bits of its territory in the eastern Himalayas, and there was massive military mobilisation on both sides following India's aggressive *Exercise Chequerboard* in 1987.

India is also in awe of China's economic growth, conceding that it would have been impossible to find the impetus for economic reform without the inspiration of China's success, rapid change in Pakistan under former Prime Minister Nawaz Sharif and the fear that both neighbours could leave it behind. There is also a belief that if India has to compete internationally with China for investments and in the fields of trade and export, it would be necessary to put the border conflict on the back-burner. However, most Indian policy-makers continue to assert that China, rather than Pakistan, will be India's long-term security threat.[5]

This makes it imperative that India does not fall too far behind China economically. China's economy is growing nearly four times as fast as India's. China's exports are four times larger and the two neighbours are competing in similar products, such as textiles, leather, marine products and medium-technology machinery. The fact that China started its economic reform a decade before India is cited by India's economic reformers to silence critics, but the sense of competitiveness is real. Rao announced in Washington, somewhat ambitiously, that India was on its way to becoming the largest free market in the world, and that in the 'interest of good neighbourly relations' did not want to outstrip China's population. Despite *détente* and disengagement on the borders, China's rising defence outlay is an immediate concern for Indian strategists. India's advantages over China are a large, urban, educated elite; English as a virtual *lingua franca*; and its functional Anglo-Saxon judicial system where foreign multinationals have often won fair judgements against domestic companies. The underpinnings of Indian industry and management are Western, and there is an established and vibrant stock market. While the Indian system does have many of the faults usually associated with democracies, there is no 'one country, two systems' contradiction between its economic and political structures.

India's internal problems and threats to its long-term stability are considerable, but generally its political system is more resilient and capable of absorbing change and electoral succession. De-escalation on the borders will therefore set in motion economic competition between the world's two most populous nations. How the overall relationship develops will be greatly determined by the way China changes and how its post-Deng leadership views both the world and its own region.

Rediscovering The United States
Indian policy-makers have begun to recognise the United States as a potential friend rather than an overbearing adversary. The US too is now able to see India as a stable, major regional power with a

democratic and pluralistic system, although uneasily set near resurgent Islam and flanked by China. If not a strategic ally, India is now perceived as having security concerns in the region that converge with those of the US. The end of the Cold War has diminished the importance of security alliances and blocs and hence the size, regional power and influence of a country are determinants of where it fits in Washington's world view. A phenomenon that began in 1988, but accelerated only towards 1993, is that US policy-makers refer to India as an emerging major power.[6] The American view of India has also been affected by a growing business lobby. These influences, on the Congress and the State Department, have been reinforced by New Delhi's success – though partial as yet – in trying to create a lobby from within the Indian community in America. Numbering nearly one million now, Indian settlers in the US are mainly prosperous professionals, and several have become active in mainstream politics. India has tried to exploit the emotional potential of the Kashmir issue, particularly following certain controversial statements by US officials, to rouse this powerful constituency.[7] Their influence on US policy is an entirely new factor and is acknowledged as significant by policy-makers in Washington.[8]

India's rediscovery of America was also helped by the problems with Soviet arms supplies, the need for Western high-technology and direct investment into the economy. These changes and increasing disillusionment with Moscow ultimately resulted in the watershed event of January 1991 when, in the run-up to the Gulf War, India opened refuelling facilities to US military aircraft. This led to a flurry of delegations between the two governments and even the militaries, resulting in what was seen as a highly successful visit by Rao to Washington in May 1994. Some contact had been established as far back as 1987 with the visit of the then US Secretary of Defense Caspar Weinberger followed by his successor Frank Carlucci in 1988. But, necessarily, discussions were confined to diplomatic niceties and possibilities of US sales of an advanced jet trainer for the Indian Air Force and collaboration in India's plans to manufacture the LCA. Then, in 1991, US Air Force General Claude M. Kickleighter visited India and proposed extensive training as well as academic exchanges between the two militaries. This was followed by a high-profile visit by Indian Army chief General S. F. Rodrigues to Washington in August 1991. The government's view of these exchanges was articulated by Rao at the Army's biennial area commanders' conference in New Delhi. He noted how the professional-to-professional relations had achieved much more than the politicians had been able to do in decades. Post-Gulf War, the list of visits of US officials to India and vice versa reads like the 'Who's Who' of top military personnel, and the two navies have even held a joint exercise, albeit a small one.

Broadly, trade, economics, commonly shared perceptions of regional stability and the threat of expanding militant Islam will be areas of agreement between India and the US in the near future. But the areas of disagreement are vast and capable of damaging the entire relationship. US urgency in pushing its non-proliferation agenda in the subcontinent, its determination to curb India's missile programme, and a general lack of sensitivity among US policy-makers towards the dynamics of Indian politics, will continue to be sizeable hurdles. It would be difficult for the US to ignore the interests of Pakistan: not only is it a long-term ally but there is much goodwill towards Pakistan in the foreign-policy, intelligence and defence establishments that, for decades, used fellow Pakistani professionals as active partners in the Cold War generally and during the Afghan campaign in particular. The US is also suspicious of India's aggressive efforts to establish a regional *modus vivendi* with Iran.

In the 1993–94 period, even as the economic relationship has blossomed (there was more US investment in India in 1994 than in the previous 40 years), serious tension remained. This was caused almost entirely by contentious statements made by key US officials, including President Clinton, on issues such as Kashmir, human rights and nuclear proliferation. However, each time a storm arose in the press and parliament, the Rao government deliberately played down the controversy. The new India needs both the goodwill and the investment of the US and the West, and has already demonstrated an inclination to make a few adjustments in policy and public postures towards that end. But, given the demands of domestic politics, it is unlikely that an Indian government can survive after making visible concessions on the nuclear and Kashmir questions. The key factors determining India's developing relationship with the US will be Washington's ability to find a sustainable balance between what it thinks is politically correct in its South Asia policy and what would be popularly acceptable in the region. On the Indian side, the factor that might determine the future of the nation, and the entire gamut of change it is going through, will also decide the fate of the relationship. That factor, clearly, is the appearance of tangible benefits of economic reform within a reasonable period of time.

Redefining Relations With Russia
Despite attempts to maintain the arms, ammunition and spares pipe-line, Indian policy-makers are resigned to the demise of the security relationship with Russia. They are also resigned to a change in the complicated, unusual, but highly beneficial trade relationship between the two countries. Even more than arms supplies, India is damaged by the loss of a strategic partner. The Soviets could always be relied on to provide political support at multilateral fora, particularly at the UN on the issue of Kashmir. Now, with Russia generally willing to agree with Washington, India can no longer take for granted a Russian veto on Kashmir resolutions. A rude shock, and a pointer to the changed equations, came in 1993 as, under US pressures, Russia reneged on the old agreement signed by its space hardware manufacturing company, Glavkosmos, to supply India with technology for cryogenic engines to be used in India's ongoing polar satellite launch vehicle (PSLV) programme. The deal has now been reduced to the supply of some engines, but no technology. The new Russia also supports the idea of a nuclear-free zone in South Asia, which runs counter to India's efforts to prevent such a regionalisation of the nuclear issue. In the recent past, India has been further irritated by Russian offers to sell arms to Pakistan on a commercial basis.

Yet there are possibilities that India and Russia will discover new common concerns and interests. One of these is trade. In time India could become a reliable supplier of reasonably priced consumer goods to Russia. If and when Russia stabilises and industry resumes normal working, India could continue to be a major buyer of Russian weaponry. Russian policy-makers have already begun to see the enormous commercial scope of expanding a modified security and technology relationship with India. During Rao's visit in June–July 1994, the two countries formalised agreements to set up joint ventures in the field of civil and military aviation. Of particular importance is the $13.5m joint venture shared by India's HAL and Industrial Credit and Investment Company of India (ICICI) and Russia's Moscow Aircraft Production Organisation, Mikoyan Design Bureau, and Rosvoorouzhenie, the armament export company, to service and upgrade Soviet-origin aircraft operated by India and third-world countries. Russian Deputy Prime Minister Yuri Yarov, on a visit to India in summer 1994, talked of reviving the Soviet proposal to build a safeguarded 2000MW nuclear power plant in Tamil Nadu, besides finding ways to continue business in the fields of space and nuclear science 'without violating international regimes and agreements'. Plans to set up engine overhaul plants for MiG-29s and for the upgrade of T-72 tanks are also being finalised. India is one of the largest successful users of Russian weaponry, and thus a vital market for the future.

In 1992, during Yeltsin's New Delhi visit, the two governments arrived at an amicable solution to the vexed issue of old Soviet debts to India. And even in the post-Cold War world, there are some common security concerns, largely regarding instability in the Central Asian region. Russia's worry about resurgent, militant Islam and instability injected by the leftover *mujaheddin* in neighbouring Afghanistan is understandable, particularly in the context of the developments in Tajikistan; while India faces growing fundamentalism in Kashmir, bordering Central Asia. In the joint declaration signed at the end of Rao's Moscow visit, the expression of shared concern for the stability and survival of multi-ethnic and multi-linguistic societies underlined the new convergence of interests. Pakistan, which sent its Foreign Minister to Moscow immediately after Rao, was the first to acknowledge this development.

Until the communist collapse, the Indo-Soviet relationship prospered because of the need for a balance against the West, and shared security and geopolitical concerns. The new Indo-Russian relationship will have to be based primarily on business interests, and coloured only marginally by geopolitics and security.

Domestic Constraints And Regional Ambitions
Independent India has had a deep desire for both regional power and international status. In the past, the Indian sense of belonging to global regimes was stimulated by the Nehru doctrine, effectively backed by his personality – Indira Gandhi only followed in his footsteps. This consisted of aggressive espousal of non-alignment as well as other political and ethical causes such as disarmament, the Palestinian issue and South African apartheid. The changing post-Cold War world has taken most of these sounding-boards away from India. Its stature has been further diminished by its continuing internal and economic problems. Indira Gandhi's policy of opposing all foreign intervention in the region and reserving for India the exclusive right to intervene if absolutely necessary, has now become obsolete. India's more inward-looking foreign policy in recent years is partly a result of these internal and international changes, although the absence of the Nehru–Gandhi dynasty has certainly been felt. Nehru, Indira and Rajiv Ghandi all saw themselves as leaders of international standing and commanded a presence to justify such

aspirations; their successors do not have the same glamour, or the wish for it. The Rao government's economic reform has brought some international focus back to India, but there are no real signs that the policy-making establishment might again turn activist internationally or regionally.

The failure of SAARC has denied India even a regional stage. There are some stirrings of activism on more contemporary issues, such as the environment or international patents and GATT proposals, but in the overall policy context these are marginal. Given its internal and economic concerns, India is likely to be cautious in the foreseeable future, striving to contain itself within its geographical boundaries and rebuilding its economy. Rao's style of diplomacy can only be described as pragmatic, practical and low-key, lacking the ambition and drive of the past. However, there is a substantive change mainly aimed at India's immediate bread-and-butter concerns rather than image-building, precisely because India's new leadership is not encumbered by the old ideological and doctrinal burdens. In fact, it was able to make major departures from past positions to improve relations with Israel and open out to South Africa as early as winter 1992, and after initial hesitation even to do business with the junta in Burma – steps that may have been unthinkable to Nehru–Gandhi followers. Regionally, however, the new India finds itself in a trajectory where, if its leaders had the foresight, it could slowly break free from Pakistan. By virtue of its size, power, stability and the interest in its economy, India would benefit from a policy of benign neglect of regional irritants while dealing directly with the great powers in a truly global and bilateral context. India does not gain by linking its relationship with the great powers, particularly the US, to its problems with Pakistan, and if it is to become respected internationally, its policy-makers will have to distance themselves from their traditional obsession with Pakistan.

India's main foreign-policy concern will be the new international pressures and opprobrium that the Kashmir violence and human-rights abuses by its security forces have brought. As one of the more vocal founders of the UN Commission on Human Rights, these are, for India, morally embarrassing and politically damaging. The Kashmir crisis could foreshadow India's isolation from the Islamic world, especially if the communal divide grows domestically. Some efforts to counter this have been visible, such as attempts to reach out to the OIC countries, particularly Iran. Improved relations between India and Iran stem from Rao's Teheran visit in autumn 1993, followed by External Affairs Minister Dinesh Singh in February 1994. Iran played a key role in persuading Pakistan to drop its motion at the UN Human Rights Convention in Geneva censuring India for its human-rights record in Kashmir. Unlike the other OIC countries, Iran has also lately adopted a remarkably detached policy towards Kashmir. It is likely that, cut out by the West, the Iranians are showing a new pragmatism in their foreign policy, evinced in their search for new allies. But it is too early for India to count this among its more durable gains.

Yet, along with the thaw with China, this is seen in Islamabad as an effort to out-flank Pakistan and isolate it from its two close friends within the region. From the Indian point of view, the attempts to reach out to the OIC countries are intended more to end its own isolation within the larger geopolitical landmass. But India also has to pay greater attention to its immediate neighbourhood, and it still endeavours to play a more benevolent role within SAARC, despite its smaller neighbours' suspicions.

CONCLUSION

Almost a half-century after India's first Prime Minister Jawaharlal Nehru made his famous 'tryst with destiny' speech to mark the birth of a free India, the country is making a break with the past; and much of the movement, ironically, is away from the path on which he had set India. Some of this is pragmatic and positive, such as the economic changes; some unavoidable, such as the foreign policy; but some fraught with danger, particularly the growing forces of communalism and casteism. The effects of these will be felt not merely among India's own people, but also regionally, and, more generally, in the international community.

Economically, with its 250m-strong – and growing – middle class, India has the potential to become a major market. But if the world, particularly the West, were to help India in its quest for an open economy and political stability, the rewards could be more than economic. It could lead to the emergence of a new, growing and confident India in a region fraught with uncertainties. Located east of Iran, west of China and south of the Central Asian and Afghan region, India is a nation in which the West should have vital stakes.

With a population of 900m, India is already the world's second largest market, and by 2030 will have the world's largest population. Its huge middle class is familiar with the Anglo-Saxon world. India's business leaders and administrators are much more in touch with Western systems of governance and judicial process. Even ideologically, if the West wishes to persuade the economically growing states of East Europe and Eastern Asia that democracy would be good for them, it is imperative that it supports India in its complicated experiment of economic reform within an existing democracy. What is required now is a policy of incentives, or positive conditionalities, rather than minor penalties over trade-policy differences or sanctions in technology export that achieve little, but become major irritants in the West's relationship with India. The danger is that if economic change is not managed well, if the social conflict, communal as well as casteist, is not controlled effectively, if regional imbalances are not checked and reversed, India could indeed evolve into a Hindu nationalist, nuclear-armed, militaristic, isolationist and insecure nation.

The world's view of India needs to be revised; in such drastically changed circumstances, some of the old rules of engagement may no longer apply. In its impatience to set things 'right' in South Asia, the West, particularly the US, tends to follow certain fixed policies. In the case of countries such as China, the Philippines, South Korea and Thailand, it is possible, although not always easy, for the West to extract favourable commitments with a mixture of the carrot and the stick. But India has its own parliament, judiciary and media, no matter how faulty or strained these institutions may be. Any obtrusive meddling in policy-making will be counter-productive, as Washington now seems to have acknowledged. Pressure and persuasion will have to be inconspicuous and it will be in the West's interests subtly to assist both democratic institutions and economic reform in India. This will go a long way towards strengthening confidence and stability in the whole region, reducing social tensions and diverting popular attention from old caste, communal, national or subnational prejudices to more constructive pursuits.

India is becoming a harder, more selfish and pragmatic entity. No longer encumbered by leaders besotted by larger-than-life images of themselves on the international stage, the new India is inclined to look at the world in terms of its own interest. It is losing the habit of sticking to ideological postures on global issues, illustrated by its revised policies towards Israel and South Africa. It will also be an India not dominated by a uniform political thought or party. With the relative decline of the Congress Party and the personality cult of the old days, India will become a much more federal entity, as the framers of its Constitution intended. There are obviously dangers of a fractious power structure resulting in administrative chaos, as different parties and groups govern different regions of the country. But this shift from the Congress-dominated past could prove to be a positive factor by satisfying regional political aspirations and lessening local pressures. Contrary to myths built up in the past, such decentralisation of political power will not lead to a weakening of India's instinct for self-preservation.

As demonstrated in Punjab and now in Kashmir, the new India will fight as hard and ruthlessly as ever to put down separatism. Internally, Kashmir will be its most serious long-term threat, followed by Hindu–Muslim tensions, particularly as, on a broader ideological level, one complicates the other. Pakistan's case is that since Kashmir has a Muslim majority, its accession to the Islamic national entity is a natural step in the 'unfinished business of Partition'. India asserts that there is no oddity in a Muslim-majority province existing within a larger, secular, if mainly Hindu, entity. The Hindu revivalist has always argued that the Indian Muslim is not a patriotic Indian, is not impressed by secularism and thus does not deserve it. Anything that seems like a capitulation to Islamic pressures on Kashmir weakens secular forces in India, provides substance to the BJP propaganda of Muslim disloyalty, and has long-term consequences for Hindu–Muslim relations in the country. Most of the other separatist demons have already been exorcised, although some still linger: the Sri Lankan separatists, led by the Liberation Tigers of Tamil Eelam (LTTE), who could exploit any future uncertainty in India's Tamil Nadu (the southern Indian coastal state has 55m Tamils, compared to 10m in Sri Lanka); and the remnants of several north-eastern tribal insurgencies, particularly the Nagas, still exist in northern Burma. But compared to Kashmir, these are relatively minor problems. Similarly, a consistent and long-term approach will have to be evolved to counter politically the threat of communalism.

Internationally, the new pragmatism in economics and some aspects of foreign policy may not be immediately reflected in the manner India relates to the West. This is partly because several of the new politically influential groups and regional parties are fundamentally suspicious of the West. It would be hard enough for Indian leaders to give their economics a Westward tilt, but they could not be seen to be compromising on security issues, whether over Kashmir or the nuclear question. India can progress with the kind of change the West might welcome on economic policy as long as it does not seem to be forced and that India's sovereignty and strategic interests are not adversely affected. While pressure on China on the human-rights issue or a clear barter on preferential trade in exchange for concessions on domestic policies are possible, in India, democratic constraints will rule out such pragmatism in foreign policy. The perils of the world misreading economic changes as signals of political compliance can be serious, as is evident from the outcry provoked by US statements made in 1993–94 on Kashmir, human rights and trade-related disputes.

The threats to India's stability would emanate from the rapidly changing internal political equations and the altered electoral calculus. The recent communal and caste tensions have redrawn the lines along which votes were divided in the past and in this seeds of discord could lie. A divided polity could result in split verdicts in future elections, at best constricting the government's decision-making ability, but at worst bringing India back to the debilitating listlessness of 1989–91. A crucial question is whether India's current and future leaders have the political adroitness to adapt to coalition politics. It will not be easy, given the ideological polarisation between rival parties and deep animosities among key leaders at the intra-party level.

Since Independence, India's foreign, security and economic policies generally followed a consistent pattern. For its neighbours, India's growing confidence and stability would be a welcome development. As a major buyer of their goods and services, India could lead the subcontinent towards its own rewards in terms of trade, tourism and security. A more confident, yet less adventurist, India would find it easier to settle economic and environment issues with its immediate neighbours, whether it is the question of sharing river waters with Bangladesh or joint exploitation of water resources with Nepal. The fate of economic reform undertaken in the region could be closely linked to the way India evolves.

Meanwhile, international peacekeeping may be a route back to the world stage. Since the 1950s, India has been a significant contributor to UN peacekeeping efforts and has recently made large contributions in Cambodia and Somalia. India's history of separatist insurgencies gives it tactical experience that can be used internationally. India would also continue to press for a restructuring of the UN Security Council while seeking a permanent seat for itself.

In the post-Cold War world, where per capita incomes and trade surpluses, rather than the size of nuclear arsenals, have become the denominators of national stature, India is reshaping its future, politically, economically and even ideologically. Its constitutional founding fathers were visionaries with a competitive streak. They believed that they were embarking on a path ideologically superior to that of both major neighbours – China with its communism; and Pakistan which chose Islamic nationalism. India's choice of parliamentary democracy and liberal constitution, despite abject poverty, lack of infrastructure and other problems typical of post-colonial societies, was an audacious experiment. Equally, the effort to usher in economic and social change within democratic parameters is unprecedented. None of the other new Asian economic tigers has built industrialised economies within a pluralistic and democratic framework. This gives India a certain advantage, in that there is no fundamental contradiction between the direction of its economic thrust, political system and security doctrine. The deftness with which Indian leadership handles Kashmir, and its ability to achieve reasonably broad consensus on crucial national issues, will determine the strength, stability and confidence of India in the future.

Notes

Introduction
[1] Economist Raj Krishna in one of his lectures in the late 1970s argued that no matter what happens to the economy, the trend growth rate in India will be 3.5%.
[2] This expression is used by Stephen P. Cohen in *The Indian Army: Its Contribution to the Development of a Nation* (New Delhi: Manohar Publications, 1990).
[3] *Annual Report* (New Delhi: Indian Ministry of Defence, 1987–88).
[4] For an excellent assessment of Indian strategic thinking, see George Tanham, 'Indian Strategic Culture', *The Washington Quarterly*, Winter, 1992.

Chapter I
[1] *The World Bank Annual Report* (WashingtonDC: The World Bank, 1993).
[2] For instance, the percentage rise in the circulation of *The Economic Times* (with editions in New Delhi, Calcutta, Bangalore, Bombay and Ahmedabad) is higher than its sister newspaper, *The Times of India*. While the circulation of *The Economic Times* rose from 120,577 in July–December 1991 to 191,307 in July–December 1993, that of *The Times of India* has risen from 601,314 to 677,722 in the same period. Similarly, the circulation of *Business Today*, launched in January 1992, rapidly reached 90,000 while that of its sister magazine *India Today* has marginally fallen from 355,000.
[3] For details, see J. Bhagwati, *India's Economy: The Shackled Giant, Radhakrishnan Lectures* (Oxford: Clarendon Press, 1992).
[4] For details, see Subhashis Gangopadhyay, 'The Indian Awakening', *The School of Advanced International Studies Journal*, vol. 14, no. 1, Winter–Spring 1994.

[5] *Ibid.*
[6] Market capitalisation on Indian money-markets, for instance, leapt from Rs1,102,790m in July 1991 to Rs4,861,620m in July 1994.
[7] The actual Foreign Direct Investment (FDI) between 1991 and January 1994 was in excess of $1bn. The World Bank expected a cumulative inflow of direct and portfolio investment of approximately $1.2bn between 1991 and 1993–94. Together with portfolio investment, the projections have been exceeded by a wide margin. More encouragingly, FDI is growing at a rate of about $600m per year. Also, there is a narrowing gap between approvals and actual FDI, which is the most preferred form of foreign capital because it is a non-debt flow.
[8] *Statistical Outline of India, 1994–95* (Bombay: Tata Services Ltd, Department of Economics and Statistics, 1994), pp. 6, 43, 147.
[9] The Aid India Consortium, renamed the India Development Forum, is an annual meeting between the Union Finance Secretary and the nation's creditors. In July 1994, Finance Secretary Montek Singh Ahluwalia attended with a high-powered delegation of industrialists, including Ratan Tata, Mukesh Ambani, R. P. Goenka and Aditya Birla. The foreign exchange reserves were as high as $19bn and the mood was upbeat.
[10] Political implications of the stock-market scandal became grave in late 1993 when Harshad Mehta, a Bombay broker and prime suspect, publicly stated that he had paid a bribe of Rs10m in a suitcase presented to Prime Minister Rao at his residence. The charge came to nothing, but parliament was paralysed on several occasions by the opposition demanding stern action on the report of a Joint Parliamentary Committee that passed damaging strictures on several politicians, including Finance Minister Manmohan Singh.

[11] The stock-exchange capitalisation had increased from $115bn at the end of 1993 to $147bn by mid-1994. There are 6,000 active brokers in the Indian Stock Exchange and the Bombay Stock Exchange has been the best performer among Asian markets outside Japan.

[12] In 1984, the BJP won only 7.4% of the votes cast and won only two of the 229 Lok Sabha seats it contested; by 1989, it had cornered 11.4% of the votes and won 85 of the 225 seats contested; while in 1991 it managed 22.9% of the popular vote and won 119 of the 473 seats contested.

[13] Hindu insecurities were articulated soon after the subcontinent's Muslims organised themselves into the Muslim League on 30 December 1906 in Dhaka. Within months, the United Bengal Hindu Movement emerged in Bengal, and in distant Punjab Hindus formed the Punjab Hindu Mahasabha (Grand Convention). Similar organisations sprang up elsewhere and by 1913 most of them came together as the All India Hindu Mahasabha.

[14] Kirti Sing, 'Women's Rights and the Reform of Personal Laws' in *Hindus and Others: The Question of Identity in India Today*, ed. Gyanendra Pandey (India: Viking, 1993).

[15] The charge of a soft policy towards Kashmir became a central point in the Hindu nationalists' agenda shortly after Independence. Dr Shyama Prasad Mookerjee, Minister for Industries and Supplies in Nehru's cabinet, having failed to secure a total integration of Kashmir into India, left the cabinet in 1950 to organise opposition to Nehru's policies. He became the first member to sit in the opposition in the Parliament-cum-Constituent Assembly of Independent India and then became the founder president of the Bharatiya Jana Sangh (BJS, the precursor of today's BJP) in October 1951. He demanded that Jammu and Kashmir be fully integrated with the rest of India. In May 1952, he was arrested by the Central Government at Gurdaspur in Punjab. He died in controversial circumstances while in prison in Srinagar, the capital of Kashmir, and still personifies the BJP's Kashmir policy.

[16] This philosophy was elaborated in M. S. Golwalkar's *Bunch of Thoughts* (New Delhi: Saraswati Pratashan, 1958). Golwalkar, one of the founding fathers of the RSS, argued that the creation of Pakistan was the 'first successful step of the Muslims in the 20th century to realise their 1,200-year dream of completing the subjugation of India'. Pakistan, he warned, was only to be the springboard for launching further subversion in India.

[17] Even a prominent young Muslim member of Rajiv Gandhi's cabinet, Arif Mohammed Khan, resigned in protest against this appeasement of fundamentalists. He became a key leader of the coalition that later came to power, unseating Gandhi's Congress.

[18] The BJP election manifesto, 1992, BJP Headquarters, New Delhi.

[19] Ramesh Menon, 'Coping with Peace', *India Today*, 15 July 1988, pp. 88–91.

Chapter II

[1] Zuheto Swu, a former Naga underground self-styled general, later rose to become a deputy inspector general in the paramilitary Border Security Force and was one of its most highly decorated officers. See Ramesh Menon, 'Nagaland: Vignettes of a Changing Land', *India Today*, 31 July 1989, pp. 66–69.

[2] Author's interview with Vanlalzari, the former personal secretary of the inspector general of police (IGP). The IGP was assassinated and she was sentenced to ten years imprisonment for complicity in the police chief's murder by the insurgents. She was

released under the amnesty clause in the peace accord.

[3] The groups leading the Assam movement came to power as a result of the election following the accord. But they were gripped by corruption and dissensions and lost the next election, bringing the Congress Party back into power. For further reading on how the Indian state tackled insurgencies in the north-east, see Nirmal Nibedon, *Nagaland: The Night of the Guerrillas* (New Delhi: Lancer, 1981); *Mizoram, The Dagger Brigade* (New Delhi: Lancer); and *Northeast: The Ethnic Explosion* (New Delhi: Lancer). Also see Shekhar Gupta, 'Ethnic Conflict and State Security in South Asia: India's Punjab Crisis', Occasional Paper for ACDIS (Program in Arms Control, Disarmament and International Security, University of Illinois), January 1988.

[4] According to Indian Home Ministry figures, in 1990 Punjab violence accounted for 4,920 lives. In 1991 this figure was up to 6,088. In 1992, it was 3,883, with as many as 2,113 terrorists being killed. In March 1993, the figure stood at 362 with a further decline in subsequent months.

Chapter III

[1] Perhaps the only notable exception in the recent past is the 1987 *Exercise Brasstacks*, which almost started another India and Pakistan war and where the military seems to have taken matters in its own hands while keeping the government in the dark.

[2] In the Indian Parliament's *Second Report of the Standing Committee on Defence* (1994–95), MPs demanded that the 'report of the Committee on Defence Expenditure be made public as early as possible' and chided that 'a little more openness even in the matter relating to defence will not militate against national interest'.

[3] *World Military Expenditures and Arms Transfers, 1990* (Washington DC: US Arms Control and Disarmament Agency, 1991).

[4] Jasjit Singh 'Trend in Defence Expenditure', *Asian Strategic Review (1992–93)* p. 33, published by the Institute for Defence and Strategic Analyses, 1994.

[5] *Second Report of Standing Committee on Defence* (1994–95), pp. 12–13.

[6] *Ibid.*

[7] Saritha Rai, 'Aviation: Wanted a Foreign Match', *India Today*, 31 January 1994, pp. 66–69.

[8] *Ibid.*

[9] Interview with Abdul Kalam, *India Today*, 15 April 1994.

[10] *Ibid.*

[11] George Perkovich 'Counting the Cost of the Arms Race', *Foreign Policy*, no.85, Winter 1991–92.

[12] Major General D. Som Dutt, *India and the Bomb,* Adelphi Paper 30 (London: IISS, 1966), and General K. Sundarji, *Blind Men of Hindoostan* (New Delhi: UBSPD, 1993).

[13] See, for instance, Brigadier V. K. Nair (retired), *Nuclear India* (New Delhi: Lancers, 1992), which estimates that India would need a total of 132 nuclear bombs to provide an effective deterrent against both China and Pakistan. A total of 60 bombs would clearly give India a second-strike capability over at least Pakistan.

[14] On 3 August 1994, Reuters reported the Indian Ambassador to Kuwait, Prem Singh, as saying: 'We have offered some training vacancies at our academies'.

[15] Saritha Rai 'Aviation', pp. 66–69.

Chapter IV

[1] The claim was first made by investigative reporter Seymour M. Hersh, 'On the Nuclear Edge', *New Yorker*, 29 March 1993, pp. 56–73, and later discussed in detail by William E. Burrows and Robert Windrem, *Critical Mass* (New York: Simon and Schuster, 1994). See also the 1994

Occasional Paper, *Conflict Prevention and Confidence Building Measures in South Asia: The 1990 Crisis*, published by the Henry L. Stimson Centre, Washington DC, following a discussion among various US officials who dealt with the crisis in the presence of some Indian and Pakistani officials. This report repudiated the claims of the threat of a nuclear war in 1990.

[2] Interview with the author, Moscow, January 1990.

[3] Interview with Harinder Baweja in *India Today*, 15 March 1994.

[4] See John Ward Anderson, 'Pakistan Resumes Aid to Kashmiris', *The Washington Post*, May 1994.

[5] Former Army Chief K. Sundarji told *India Today* (15 May 1988) that China was India's main threat for the future while Pakistan could be dealt with *en passant*. See also Jasjit Singh's article in *Asian Strategic Review (1992–93)*, published by the Institute of Defence Studies and Analyses, New Delhi.

[6] Speech delivered by Lee Hamilton to Asia Society, July 1994.

[7] Controversy arose following a statement by Robin Raphel, US Assistant Secretary of State for South Asia, in October 1993 questioning the validity of the Instrument of Accession on the basis of which Jammu and Kashmir, a princely state in colonial India, joined the Indian union after the Partition of the subcontinent.

[8] Author's interviews, Washington DC, June 1994.

Printed by Halstan & Co. Ltd., Amersham, Bucks., England